The collapse of the Soviet Union and the emergence of fifteen independent states on its former territory is one of the most momentous developments of the twentieth century. In this volume, leading scholars from the United States, Canada, and Russia examine the forces that underlay the rise of national movements in the Soviet Union and their challenge to the stability and territorial integrity of the Soviet state.

The authors offer new arguments concerning the link between political structure and nationalism, finding that Soviet policies designed to eliminate national distinctiveness frequently had the unintended result of creating new national identities. With the pursuit of perestroika and glasnost, such identities became a potent political force, impelling the Soviet leadership to grapple with the growing tension between demands for regional sovereignty and the preservation of central economic and political control. The contributors show how, in the course of this struggle, the international system often played a critical role. Non-Russian national movements sought to expand their ties to Europe or Asia even as they pursued independence from Moscow. But it was the transformation of Russian national consciousness, and the emergence of a Russian state which disassociated itself from the legacy of empire, which played a decisive role in the collapse of the center. The progressive weakening of central institutions and the emergence of increasingly assertive sovereign states was accelerated by the failed coup of August 1991.

Presenting a broad and timely analysis of the national dimension of politics after perestroika, this book is essential reading for all those seeking to understand the complexities underlying the demise of the Soviet state, as well as the emergence of new states actively engaged in defining their national identities at home and abroad.

D1416066

FROM UNION TO COMMONWEALTH: NATIONALISM AND SEPARATISM IN THE SOVIET REPUBLICS

Cambridge Soviet Paperbacks: 6

Cambridge Soviet Paperbacks is a new initiative in publishing on the Soviet Union. The series focuses on the economics, international relations, politics, sociology, and history of the Soviet and revolutionary periods.

The idea behind the series is the identification of gaps for upper-level surveys or studies falling between the traditional university press monograph and most student textbooks. The main readership will be students and specialists, but some "overview" studies in the series will have broader appeal.

Publication will in every case be simultaneously in hardcover and paperback.

Cambridge Soviet Paperbacks

From union to commonwealth: Nationalism and separatism in the Soviet republics

Edited by

GAIL W. LAPIDUS
Professor of Political Science, University of California at Berkeley and Chair, Berkeley–Stanford Program in Soviet Studies

AND VICTOR ZASLAVSKY
Professor, Department of Sociology, Memorial University of Newfoundland

WITH PHILIP GOLDMAN
Ph.D. Candidate, Department of Political Science, University of California at Berkeley

CAMBRIDGE
UNIVERSITY PRESS

Published by the Press Syndicate of the University of Cambridge
The Pitt Building, Trumpington Street, Cambridge CB2 1RP
40 West 20th Street, New York, NY 10011–4211, USA
10 Stamford Road, Oakleigh, Victoria 3166, Australia

© Cambridge University Press 1992

First published 1992

Printed in Great Britain at the University Press, Cambridge

A catalogue record for this book is available from the British Library

Library of Congress cataloguing in publication data

From union to commonwealth: nationalism and separatism in the Soviet
republics / edited by Gail W. Lapidus and Victor Zaslavsky with Philip
Goldman.
  p.   cm.   (Cambridge Soviet paperbacks: 6)
Includes index.
ISBN 0 521 42716 9 (hardback) ISBN 0 521 41706 6 (paperback)
1. Nationalism – Soviet Union. 2. Minorities – Soviet Union.
3. Soviet Union – Ethnic relations. 4. Perestroïka – Soviet Union.
I. Lapidus, Gail Warshofsky. II. Zaslavsky, Victor, 1937– .
III. Goldman, Philip (Philip Sanders) IV. Series.
DK33.N28 1992
305.8′00947–dc20 92–28990 CIP
ISBN 0 521 41706 6 hardback
ISBN 0 521 42716 9 paperback

CE

Contents

Notes on the contributors

Leokadia Mikhailovna Drobizheva is a leading Russian specialist on national identities and national movements in the Soviet Union. A research scholar and former deputy director of the USSR Academy of Sciences' Institute of Ethnography in Moscow, she has written a number of books and articles in Russian on religion in the USSR, ethnocultural traditions, and the role of the intelligentsia in national movements.

Philip Goldman is a doctoral candidate in the Department of Political Science at the University of California, Berkeley. He has written on the structure of Soviet federalism and is co-author of a forthcoming article on the evolution of the foreign ministries in the Soviet republics.

Gail Warshofsky Lapidus is Professor of Political Science at the University of California, Berkeley and Chair of the Berkeley-Stanford Program in Soviet Studies. The author of numerous articles on Soviet nationality questions, her publications also include *Women in Soviet Society: Equality, Development, and Social Change* and most recently, as joint editor, *The Soviet System in Crisis*.

Galina Vasil'evna Starovoiteva is a leading research scholar on nationality issues, and is currently an adviser to Russian President Boris Yeltsin. She is the author of *Etnicheskaia gruppa v sovremennom Sovetskom gorode* (The Ethnic Group in the Contemporary Soviet City) and of many other articles on the nationalities issue in the Soviet Union. Starovoiteva has also served as a research associate at the USSR Academy of Sciences' Institute of Ethnography in Moscow, and as a deputy of both the USSR Supreme Soviet and the Supreme Soviet of the Russian Federation.

Ronald Grigor Suny is Professor of History at the University of Michigan, Ann Arbor. His publications include *The Baku Commune, 1917–1918, Armenia in the Twentieth Century, The Making of the Georgian Nation,* as editor, *Transcaucasia, Nationalism, and Social Change: Essays in the History of Armenia, Azerbaijan, and Georgia*, and, as joint editor, *Party, State and Society in the Russian Civil War* and *The Russian Revolution and Bolshevik Victory*.

Victor Zaslavsky is Professor of Sociology at the Memorial University of Newfoundland, Canada. He has published extensively on ethnicity in the Soviet Union, including *The Neostalinist State: Class, Ethnicity and Consensus in Soviet Society* and *Soviet-Jewish Emigration and Soviet Nationality Policy* (with R. Brym).

Preface

The dissolution of the Soviet Union in December 1991 and the emergence of fifteen independent states on its territory mark the end not only of the Soviet system itself but also of a centuries-long process of state-building that created the Russian empire. In the process of preserving and extending this empire, the Soviet state unwittingly stimulated a process of nation-building among its constituent peoples, which ultimately contributed to its collapse. The papers presented in this volume are an attempt to analyze and comment on the origins, evolution, and demise of this protracted experiment. Originally presented at a panel of the World Congress of Soviet and East European Studies at Harrogate, England and repeatedly updated to keep pace with the rapid changes in the Soviet Union, they inevitably reflect the turbulence of the Soviet scene in 1990–1991. Because they were completed at different dates, they offer different judgments about the prospects of preserving some form of confederation among the former Soviet republics.

The authors and the senior editors owe a special debt to Philip Goldman, who not only co-authored the introduction and dealt with the intricacies of translating the Russian papers but was instrumental in performing the many editorial tasks that transform these papers into a book. We would also like to thank James Chavin for his assistance with the translations, and Kira Reoutt and Kiran Kamboj for their tireless work on successive drafts.

We are especially grateful to Michael Holdsworth of the Cambridge University Press for his encouragement and wise counsel throughout the difficult gestation period of this volume.

Gail W. Lapidus
Victor Zaslavsky

Berkeley, March 1992

Glossary

autonomous republic: the second highest territorial unit, after the union republic, in the Soviet federation.

Belarus: the name adopted by the Belorussian Soviet Socialist Republic after the breakup of the USSR in 1991.

Bishkek: formerly the Soviet city of Frunze, and capital of Kyrgyzstan (renamed in 1991).

CPSU: Communist Party of the Soviet Union.

Commonwealth of Independent States: The name given to the loosely organized political entity that emerged after the demise of the Soviet Union in December 1991.

Ekaterinburg: formerly the Soviet city of Sverdlovsk, renamed in 1991.

glasnost: Russian for "openness," or public disclosure, the term referred to policies aimed at removing constraints on press criticism of Soviet political organs. Gradually, it came to embody a broader notion of political and social freedoms, such as freedom of speech and religion.

khozraschet: Russian for economic accounting, the term refers to the attempts by the Gorbachev leadership to devolve partial financial responsibility from the all-Union organs to the republics and enterprises.

Kyrgyzstan: formerly the Kirghiz Soviet Socialist Republic, renamed in 1991.

Moldova: formerly the Moldovian Soviet Socialist Republic, renamed in 1991.

Nagorno-Karabakh: largely populated by Armenians, this autonomous region within Azerbaijan became the locus of violent clashes between Christian Armenians and Muslim Azeris both before and after the Soviet breakup. The region is completely surrounded by Azeri territory, but sought political and economic independence from the Azeri state.

Nhzhnii Novgorod: formerly the Soviet city of Gorky, renamed in 1991.

nomenklatura: a list of individuals selected by higher Party officials for eligibility for Party and state positions.

perestroika: commonly translated as "restructuring," the term came to embody Soviet President Mikhail Gorbachev's attempts to reform the USSR's economic and political system.

RSFSR: Russian Soviet Federated Socialist Republic (also Russian Federation).

St Petersburg: formerly the Soviet city of Leningrad, this pre-revolutionary name was readopted after a referendum by city voters approved the change in the summer of 1991.

Samara: formerly the Soviet city of Kuibyshev, renamed in 1991.

Serglyev Posad: formerly the Soviet city of Zagorsk, renamed in 1991.

sliianie: Russian for "merging," the term refers to the notion that the Soviet nationalities would gradually lose their distinctiveness as their economic development progressed.

Tiflis: formerly the Soviet city of Tbilisi, the capital of Georgia.

Turkmenistan: the name adopted by the Turkmen SSR (also Turkmenia) in 1991.

Tver: formerly the Soviet city of Kalinin, renamed in 1991.

union republic: the highest territorial unit of the Soviet federation. Before the secession of the three Baltic republics in 1991, there were fifteen union republics in the USSR. These were the Armenian Soviet Socialist Republic (SSR), the Azeri SSR, the Belorussian SSR, the Estonian SSR, the Georgian SSR, the Kazakh SSR, the Kirghiz SSR, the Latvian SSR, the Lithuanian SSR, the Moldavian SSR, the Russian Soviet Federated Socialist Republic, the Ukrainian SSR, the Uzbek SSR, the Tajik SSR, and the Turkmen SSR.

USSR: Union of Soviet Socialist Republics.

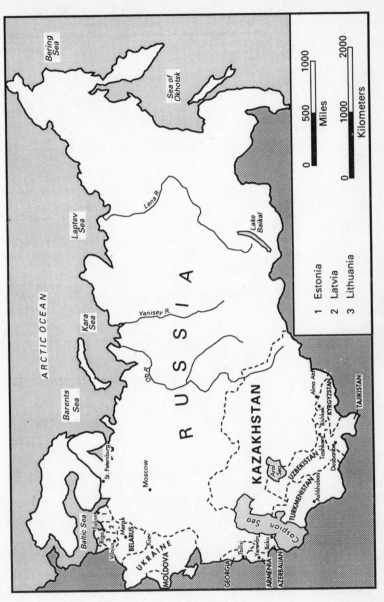

The Soviet Successor States

1 Introduction: Soviet federalism – its origins, evolution, and demise

PHILIP GOLDMAN, GAIL LAPIDUS AND
VICTOR ZASLAVSKY

The changing nature of Soviet federalism

For decades, obsessive Soviet preoccupation with external security spurred the development of a massive military establishment as well as a gigantic military-industrial complex to support it. But ultimately the primary threat to the stability and territorial integrity of the USSR came from within. The failure of the coup attempt of August 1991 accelerated a process of disintegration which was already under way, and gave new impetus to the demands for independence by many of the constituent republics of the former union. Disintegration now threatens the Commonwealth of Independent States itself, and ethnic minorities in Georgia, Moldova, and Russia are asserting their own claims to statehood.

This volume focuses on the fundamental sources of the Soviet Union's transition from a stable and highly centralized state to a system in chaos, as well as on the forces that will shape the post-coup future of what was once the Soviet Union. Three issues are of key importance: the relationship of the union republics to the center, the relationship of ethnic minorities to the republics in which they reside, and the future political and economic role of the Russian Federation. These relationships, in turn, have been profoundly shaped by the nature of the Soviet system, and particularly by the initial decision to organize the Soviet state on the basis of a hierarchy of ethnoterritorial units.

The historical circumstances which prompted the Bolsheviks to organize the Soviet state according to the principle of national-territorial autonomy have produced outcomes neither intended nor anticipated by its creators.[1] Marxist-Leninist doctrine assumed that the objective laws of history guaranteed mankind's progress towards the unification and eventual fusion of nations. In practice, however, the Bolsheviks ultimately fell back on a federal model in their search for

1

new forms of political organization, a model Lenin had rejected prior to the seizure of power. During Lenin's lifetime, this approach enabled them to preserve the strong and centralized multiethnic state deemed necessary to the final goal of world revolution. In subsequent decades, it facilitated the maintenance of the internal stability of the Soviet multiethnic empire.[2]

The introduction of the federal principle and the proclamation of the right of self-determination, dutifully preserved in all Soviet constitutions, were intended as temporary measures designed to weaken resistance to the formation of the Soviet Union among newly assertive national groups. However, as Ronald Suny and Victor Zaslavsky argue here, seven decades of Soviet nationality policies resulted in two outcomes antithetical to the officially proclaimed goals of merging nationalities and transcending ethnic distinctions. First, these policies led to the creation and emergence of nations and national identities in many communities which had not achieved ethnic consciousness by 1917. Despite policies intended to weaken or subvert national identities and loyalties, the Soviet period was also one of nation-building for many ethnic groups.

Second, Soviet nationality policies led to the creation of a federation of ethnoterritorial units organized into a complex administrative hierarchy. Ethnicity in Soviet society was institutionalized both on the individual and on group levels. On the individual level, nationality was registered on each person's internal passport, thus establishing a rigid ethnic affiliation for every citizen that passed immutably from one generation to the next. At the group level, the ethnoterritorial basis of political organization established firm links between nationality groups, their territories, and their political administrations. Consequently, the major components of the Soviet Union – its union republics – were in effect turned into peculiar forms of the "tactical nation-state."[3] Notwithstanding their far-reaching subjugation by the center, they thereby acquired the preconditions for independent existence, including their own political elites and educated middle classes, their own administratively defined territories inhabited by indigenous populations, and a continuous tradition of cultural production in their own languages.

Ernest Gellner has suggested that the Soviet Union's social and economic policies were an attempt "to endow the total society with the fluid type of organic solidarity, ensuring that ethnic-cultural boundaries within it should cease in any way to be structural markers ... The division of labor, or social complementarity, is then something pursued at the level of individuals, and avoided at the level of ethnic groups, of social subunits."[4] To this end, the Soviet regime applied a uniform developmental strategy to ethnic subjects who differed dramatically in their cultural traditions, levels of industrial development, demographic behavior, and political cultures.

This program achieved mixed results. On the one hand, the introduction of analogous institutional structures throughout the union republics and special programs for protecting the educational and occupational interests of the indigenous middle classes resulted in the emergence of large educated strata and local political elites. The social-professional structures of the titular nationalities became increasingly similar – though by no means identical – with respect to such indices as the proportions of basic social groups, as in the case of college-educated specialists.[5] On the other hand, the attempted imposition of a monolithic and uniform superstructure on an exceptionally diverse set of cultures encountered substantial resistance and made only modest inroads in many regions of the country. In important respects, Soviet policies preserved or exacerbated the developmental gap between the union republics.[6]

This system, fraught with immense contradictions, was nonetheless capable of generating compliance and maintaining internal stability as long as the central state was strong enough to control the composition and activities of local administrations, to suppress by force any attempt at organizing local nationalist movements, and to make the idea of a multiethnic empire at least tolerable for the key social groups within the non-Russian republics. Soviet policies were also, by and large, successful at integrating the diverse nationalities of the USSR into a single state so that the centrally planned economy could use the enormous natural, material, and human resources of the country to maintain extensive growth. The Soviet command-administrative system nonetheless failed to establish the conditions necessary to handle the demands of the burgeoning scientific-technological revolution. Ultimately, the exhaustion of the resources available for Soviet development and for the maintenance of the status quo undermined the state's nationality policies, and the Soviet system entered a period of sustained crisis. Perestroika was the Soviet leadership's response to this crisis, but it was a response which inadvertently exacerbated ethnic tensions.

As Gail Lapidus argues, the accession of Mikhail Gorbachev and the inauguration of reforms centered on glasnost and perestroika led to a cognitive and political revolution which irreversibly changed the nature of the national question in Soviet political life. The appearance of new and potent national movements in various parts of the Soviet Union was an unintended consequence of the "revolution from above" that was introduced by the reformist segment of the Communist Party. The internal logic of the leadership's policy changes transformed the nationalities issue from a minor problem into a major one, triggering a process of Soviet disintegration.

From the outset, far-reaching reforms designed to revitalize the Soviet system encountered resistance from the enormous Soviet bureaucracy, and were further stymied by the habitual passivity of the population at large. The latter would be the focus of Gorbachev's initial political strategy. In order to implement substantive reforms while facing resistance and sabotage by this ossified bureaucratic apparatus, the leadership sought to enlist the support of broader strata of the population. It was clear from the start that the only way to give some voice to the Soviet population at large would be to reduce the role of political coercion and to combine this with a limited democratization whose most immediate expression would be competitive elections. To enhance popular participation in the political process, the reformers renewed and broadened the anti-Stalinist campaign. Not only did it contribute to discrediting the KGB and its terroristic methods; it increasingly de-legitimated key elements of Soviet ideology and practice. During this campaign, social mobilization from above was progressively supplemented – and in some parts of the Soviet Union replaced – by a spontaneous mobilization from below.

The campaign for democratization gave birth to a whole array of new socio-political movements, foremost among them the "popular fronts." The initial goal, as envisioned by intellectuals close to the Gorbachev leadership, was to create a nationwide political movement that would not challenge the single party regime, but would support the party reformers (led by Gorbachev) against the old guard of the party-state apparatus. What emerged instead were republic popular fronts, largely based on ethnic affiliation, which ultimately turned against the all-Union leadership. While their initial programs espoused both civic and national rights, calling for democratization, pluralism, and respect for human rights, the tension between civic and ethnic orientations was often resolved so as to give precedence to national interests and aspirations over universal civic rights.

The powerful tendency for political mobilization to express itself in national movements rather than in political parties was the product of two key features of the Soviet system. First, competitive elections stimulated intense political activism primarily at the local level. Much of this early organization was spontaneous and even chaotic; after seventy years of single-party rule, no traditions of pluralist political organization at the grassroots level could be drawn upon. The new political parties lacked prior experience in formulating programs or attracting mass followings, as well as the resources to build coherent structures. Nor could they identify with and articulate the particular interests of various groups and strata since these interests were still in the process of being formed. Because the Soviet Union had evolved as a marketless formation based on nationalized property, a centrally planned economy, and a single-party political regime, it had its own principles and practices of internal differentiation and stratification. This stratification divided the population into a variety of functional groups, distributing rewards and privileges in ways that favored those groups whose activities were deemed crucial for the preservation and reproduction of the Soviet system. When this system began unravelling with the decline of the state which had been responsible for its emergence, nationality became the most potent base of mass political mobilization.

Several factors help explain this outcome. First, the ethnoterritorial structure of the Soviet system meant that the weakening of the central institutions would enhance the relative status and power of the republics. Second, shared historical grievances and threats to ethnic survival provided powerful bonds within many of them. Third, because the ruling party-state not only enjoyed a monopoly of political power, but was simultaneously responsible for economic and social development, the growing deterioration of Soviet economic and social conditions meant that discontent in the periphery would be directed against the center. Moreover, the incoherence and inner contradictions of Gorbachev's economic policies had particularly devastating consequences for republic and local officials; ever greater responsibilities were devolved upon them while at the same time they were increasingly deprived of the resources needed to deal with them. Because of the centrality of the Russian population in the Soviet empire, and the obvious Russian hegemony in the Soviet state, it was not surprising that growing discontent increasingly took the form of anti-Russian sentiments, linked in a number of cases with separatist aspirations. These emerging orientations among the non-Russian nations of the USSR in turn shaped the character of Russian nationalism.

Patterns of national assertion

The political mobilization of different national groups took a variety of forms. Any attempt at a typology of such complex social processes inevitably oversimplifies the differences between one republic and another. Still, some generalizations can be made about the common historical, cultural, and structural characteristics of the union republics that linked the goals and agendas of the various national movements.

The Baltic republics have been characterized by a strong sense of national identity, nurtured by the experience of independent existence, however brief. Culturally distinct from Russia, they considered themselves European nations, and their intellectuals felt a strong attraction to the so-called "common European home." Moreover, their geopolitical location as well as historical experience made political independence a viable proposition. Separatism was further propelled in Estonia and Latvia by the perceived threat to ethnic survival; an influx of Russian immigrants threatened to turn Estonians and Latvians into minorities within their own republics. Equally threatening in all three republics was the center's mobilization of ethnic minorities, such as Poles and Russians, against the titular nationalities in its efforts to undermine local national movements. Moreover, because these republics enjoyed a higher than average standard of living within the USSR, but were disadvantaged by comparison with Scandinavia and Europe, they could readily believe they subsidized the inefficient Soviet economy. Finally, while they embraced the general reformist project of marketization, they believed only full independence from the USSR would promote economic modernization, foreign investments in their economies, and integration with the world market. It was not surprising that these republics refused to take part in Gorbachev's March 1991 referendum on the preservation of the Soviet Union, and instead conducted polls and "pre-referendums" among their populations to demonstrate their will to secede from the union. With the failure of the coup, their full independence was finally conceded.

Georgia also shared with the Baltic republics a strong sense of national identity, and its own brief period of independent existence. Yet it is distinct from the Baltic states in a number of significant ways. Less threatened demographically than territorially by its Abkhazian and Ossetian minorities, the Georgian government has violently suppressed independence movements on its territory. Georgia's economic and geographical position is less conducive to trade with Europe than the Baltics; its trade patterns within the USSR do not demonstrate a clear "exploitation" of Georgian resources, though there is widespread resentment against Moscow's poorly conceived development of the region. Most importantly, the republic did not have the clear-cut legal claim to sovereignty enjoyed by the Baltic states due to their annexation by Stalin after the signing of the Molotov-Ribbentrop Pact, a problem which the Georgian leadership attempted to circumvent by asserting the illegitimacy of the political system itself and the coerced nature of Georgia's accession to the union.

The Central Asian republics of Uzbekistan, Turkmenistan, and Tajikistan, by contrast, have been notable for their conservatism, attachment to the union, and resistance to radical marketization and democratization. It is often argued that the cultural traditions of these republics, with their predominantly Muslim populations and the absence of past experience with national statehood, inhibit ethnic activism. But the main reason for the absence of national and separatist movements in these republics stems from the distinctive patterns of Soviet modernization as applied to the indigenous Muslim society.[7] It resulted in an unusual social structure, in which a huge educated class rested on a largely traditional society whose proportion of the rural population is close to 60 percent, and still growing. As Zaslavsky shows, the emergence of these educated classes was caused not so much by the requirements of the modern economy, but by the policies of a center seeking internal stability through the institutional isomorphism of the republics.

Consequently, the middle classes of these republics – social groups whose role in creating and promulgating nationalist ideologies and in organizing secessionist movements has traditionally been crucial – were effectively neutralized.[8] Dependent on a strong central state for redistributive economic policies, they pressed Moscow for increased subsidies, higher prices for local products, especially cotton, special aid from all-Union funds to deal with severe environmental degradation, and assistance in providing new jobs for the exploding population – not for economic or political sovereignty. Under these circumstances, ethnic activism manifested itself not in national or separatist movements, but in the archaic form of violent clashes between titular nationalities and ethnic minorities, where ethnicity served to mobilize groups in competition for scarce rewards. While these republics declared themselves independent after the coup, they remained strong supporters of an economic union that would at the very least help to stave off economic collapse, and that would ideally serve as a continuing source of capital for Central Asian development.

The other two Central Asian republics, Kirghizia and Kazakhstan, shared some of the features of their neighbors in the region, but were headed by reformist leaders more prepared to support liberalization and marketization. Both Kirghiz President Askar Akaev and Kazakh President Nursultan Nazarbayev recognized the dependence of their republics on the central treasury: Akaev faced a 6.3 billion ruble deficit for 1992, and only received a 600 million ruble subsidy from Yeltsin in 1991.[9] Yet Akaev and Nazarbayev believed that the only way out of this dependent relationship was through rapid change in the existing system, bolstered by financial and technical support from Western and Asian powers. Impressed by the economic successes of the newly industrialized economies of Asia, Nazarbayev has expressed interest in following the South Korean development model, even arguing that Kazakhstan's abundant natural resources give it an advantage over resource-poor Korea.

Azerbaijan's situation would resemble that of Central Asia were it not for the presence of Azeris in northern Iran, as well as the simmering conflict over Nagorno-Karabakh. A separatist project based on the establishment of a "Greater Azerbaijan" uniting both Soviet and Iranian territory gained some popularity among local intellectuals, and limited joint development projects were pursued with Iran. The case of the Armenian and Moldovan republics, by contrast, was closer to that of the Baltics and Georgia. Characteristically, both of these republics objected to Gorbachev's referendum on the preservation of the union. However, the small size of the republics, their lack of natural resources, and their unfavorable geopolitical situations reduced the credibility of any proposed secessionist projects and inhibited the crystallization of mass separatist movements. Even prior to the failed coup, ethnic activism was directed at attempts to solve outstanding conflicts by force.

The Slavic republics of Ukraine and Belorussia confronted a somewhat different set of challenges. Their cultural affinity with the Russians, their role in supporting Russian hegemony in the empire, and the high degree of Russification long obstructed the development of separate ethnic identities. It is notable that more Ukrainians and Belorussians entered into mixed marriages (from 33 percent to 38 percent of the total population) than any other major national group.[10] Moreover, the internal division between the heavily Russified eastern Ukraine and western Ukraine, annexed only after World War II and culturally quite different from its eastern counterpart, made the development of a cohesive republic-wide separatist movement more difficult. On the other hand, support for a powerful and sovereign Ukrainian state with its own armed forces grew rapidly and culminated in an overwhelming vote for independence in December 1991. The emergence of a new Ukrainian state will have far-reaching consequences for Ukrainian–Russian relations, for the future of any possible confederative structure, and for the broader European balance.

Perhaps the most dramatic development of recent years has been the transformation of Russian national consciousness from its traditional association with an imperial identity toward a concern with creating a Russian national state. Until quite recently, the dominant strand of Russian nationalism has been anti-Western, focusing on Russian exclusiveness, the uniqueness of the Russian historical path, and the messianic mission of the Russian people. All too often, this impulse was closely associated with the defense of the empire. But as Leokadia Drobizheva, Galina Starovoiteva, and Victor Zaslavsky demonstrate in this volume, there has been a notable shift in recent years away from the former imperial consciousness to a profound disillusionment with empire, accompanied by a widespread conversion to the ideas of liberal Russian nationalism.

The dissolution of the British empire, and French decolonization after World War II, demonstrated that when colonies become a burden and are perceived as liabilities rather than assets, a rapid change in popular attitudes towards empire may occur and the process of decolonization will encounter only limited resistance within the metropole. In the Soviet case, the explosion of anti-Russian sentiments in the non-Russian republics was largely shaped by a general dissatisfaction with the Soviet system and its declining performance. Except among the Russian settler communities in the non-Russian republics, the predominant Russian reaction to these sentiments was less an upsurge in great power chauvinism than a crystallization of Russian nationalism. The notion of a Russia free from its burdensome empire appeared to entice the Russian popular mind, and it became increasingly common for segments of the intelligentsia to envision the Russian future from the standpoint of enlightened national interest. Aleksandr Solzhenitsyn's call before the coup for the voluntary or (if necessary) forceful breakup of the Soviet Union and the creation of a new Slavic state spawned a heated debate and gave a new impulse to the diffusion of Russian national ideas.[11]

The apparent shift of attitudes in Russia does not preclude a resurgence of the historically rooted Russian imperialist mentality, particularly as the disintegration of the Soviet state brings with it challenges to the territorial integrity of Russia itself as well as appeals for assistance from Russian settler groups outside it. Furthermore, Russian nationalism is a heterogeneous ideology which embraces a variety of political orientations. Its liberal-democratic wing, which advocates cooperation with the West and a return to Russia's "European roots," stands in stark opposition to the anti-Western, "fundamentalist" strand within Russian nationalism, hostile to marketization and to individualism more broadly, and focuses on Russian exclusiveness, the uniqueness of the Russian historical path and the messianic mission of the Russian people. Such "fundamentalist" strains could readily mushroom in an atmosphere of economic breakdown or in response to a massive immigration of embittered Russians from the republics.[12]

Gorbachev and the demise of Soviet federalism

The upsurge of national consciousness and political activism triggered by the reforms confronted the Gorbachev leadership with a unique set of challenges. The task of articulating a systematic and comprehensive nationality policy that would respond to the demands for greater republic autonomy while preserving the territorial integrity of the Soviet state proved to be extremely difficult. In part, the policy failures reflected the personal limitations of the Gorbachev leadership itself and its lack of sensitivity towards the entire issue. Moreover, as Galina Starovoiteva's contribution emphasizes, the leadership never fully overcame its bureaucratic approach to the problem, which was based on a refusal to alter the arbitrarily drawn boundaries between ethno-territorial units and the hierarchical system of ethnic statehoods.[13]

Faced with the competing demands of the central apparatus and of the various republics, Gorbachev tried to accommodate the pressures for greater political and economic sovereignty by proposing a more flexible set of federal arrangements. The center's embrace of republican *khozraschet* (self-management and self-financing), which originated as a response to the Baltic demands for control over their economies, was in large part a device enabling it to transfer the provision of social services from the all-Union budget to republican governments. But the definition of *khozraschet* by various republics differed radically depending on the economic situation and particular interests of the republic in question.[14] The Baltic republics, in particular, perceived *khozraschet* as a means to accomplish a total break with the Soviet economic system through the establishment of markets for land, labor, and capital, and the creation of local currencies. They defined *khozraschet* as a temporary obligation to pay a certain percentage of their tax receipts to the central budget.

For a time, it seemed that Gorbachev's "new thinking" on the nationality question and actual Baltic developments were compatible. But by 1990, it had become clear that there were no grounds for compromise. Ethnic mobilization in the Baltic republics quickly evolved beyond an ethnic activism which sought greater autonomy within the Soviet federation to a full-fledged separatist movement. When the Gorbachev leadership rejected the demand for a speedily negotiated separation, enacted legislation which virtually precluded secession from the USSR, launched an economic blockade against Lithuania in 1990, and engaged in bloody crackdowns in Lithuania and Latvia in February 1991, it made direct confrontation between the center and the secessionist republics appear imminent.

Arguably, Gorbachev's concessions were too little, too late; approaches which might have worked previously became progressively untenable as the center's perceived rigidity encouraged radicalization in the periphery. However, an analysis of the 1989 CPSU Draft Platform on the nationalities question suggests that the impasse was more than the result of Gorbachev's slow reaction.[15] The main efforts of the Soviet leadership were directed at preserving the Soviet multiethnic state and guaranteeing that the center would continue to dominate it. As Gorbachev argued, "our party is in favor of a large and powerful federal state"[16] and his proposed reforms of the federal structure would have modified to only a limited degree the prevailing distribution of power. While the leadership acquiesced in strengthening the powers of the union republics, supporting greater ethnocultural autonomy, and granting official status to the languages of the titular nationalities of each republic, the draft Union Treaty assigned the center responsibility not only for defense, security and foreign policy, but also for "coordinating and resolving common problems in the spheres of the economy, science and culture; guaranteeing and protecting individual rights; promoting integration processes and organizing mutual assistance."[17] The leadership sought to resist the growing fragmentation along ethnic lines of central institutions like the Party and the army, and rejected demands for the creation of republic military and police forces outside central control. Even the principle of national self-determination was reformulated to shift the emphasis from secession to a "self-management which ensures the preservation of ethnic distinctiveness and presupposes a voluntary integration of the republics and other ethnic formations in order to resolve common tasks."[18]

In its efforts to resist further encroachments on its powers, the center commanded the loyalty of much of the state bureaucracy, the ruling Communist Party, the military and the coercive apparatus well into 1991. At the same time, the ideological, institutional, economic, and coercive instruments crucial for the reproduction of the system were largely eroded. Presidential decrees and Supreme Soviet directives were frequently ignored by the local governments and parliaments. The CPSU was fragmenting along political as well as ethnic lines, and segments of the military threatened to seize power to halt and reverse the disintegration of the state. The divergence of interests between the Russian and Soviet governments was aggravated by the personal antagonism between Russian President Boris Yeltsin and Gorbachev, as well as by pressures from the autonomous republics within the Russian Federation for greater sovereignty over their own affairs.

In the struggle between the center and the union republics, which Gorbachev characterized as a "war of sovereignties, a war of laws, a war for authority owing to the lack of a clarification of powers,"[19] the center increasingly sought to play the interests of ethnic minorities against those of the union republics by enhancing the political stature and role of sub-republican ethnic elites while preserving for itself the role of ultimate arbiter. In 1990, with the center's encouragement, the overwhelming majority of autonomous republics unilaterally attempted to raise their status to that of a union republic, while many ethnoterritorial units adopted declarations of sovereignty, claiming exclusive rights to their territory's natural resources. Moscow also agreed to make the autonomous republics subjects of the new Union Treaty, which in its original form would have effectively diluted the power of the fifteen union republics in the proposed new federation.

The central government also lent its support to the efforts of segments of the Russian settler communities in the Baltic republics and Moldova to resist the political claims of the titular nationalities. The leaders of the Russian "Interfront" movements in the Baltic states were closely tied to the military and KGB, and drew support from the military-industrial enterprises in these republics. Following a barrage of propaganda attacks against Baltic separatism in the central mass media, anonymous self-appointed bodies (the so-called national salvation committees) sprang up in Lithuania and Latvia in January 1991 supported by Soviet troops stationed in the region. Simultaneously, Russian migrant workers employed by the military-industrial complex, the atomic power stations, and the railroads declared a political strike calling for the dissolution of the democratically elected republican governments and the introduction of presidential rule. Gorbachev was prepared to recognize the legitimacy of the salvation committees. But the attempted crackdown backfired in the face of massive popular resistance and international criticism, and strengthened the determination to pursue independence. In the subsequent referendums conducted by the Baltic republics, the overwhelming majority of voters supported secession.

The Baltic crackdown ironically contributed to a new consolidation of democratic forces throughout the USSR, especially in the Russian Republic, and it provoked a strong Western reaction despite the concern with the Gulf War. The episode turned into a political disaster for Gorbachev, whose credibility as a reformist leader was further damaged, and it obliged him to promise that military force would not be used in settling nationality issues.

The CPSU itself was divided by national as well as political conflicts. As Lapidus notes, the myth of "internationalism" did seem to be exposed by *novoe myshlenie* (new thinking). Yet many began advocating the discredited policy of *sliianie* (merging) through the socioeconomic development of all of the republics, an approach which reduced the conflicts in the Soviet Union to the economic dimension. For example, Politburo member Alexander Dzasokhov called for a new push for internationalism to replace the current nationalist trends, as there was a need to solve problems "in unison."[20] Other Party cadres, frequently associated with the Leningrad Initiative Congress of the Russian Communist Party of the summer of 1990, advocated the explicit recognition that Russian and communist values are inextricably linked. Such Party members simultaneously pushed for the widespread proliferation of Russian national symbols and the reassertion of Russian hegemony in the Soviet Union through CPSU institutions.

The objective difficulties of designing and enforcing a new postcoup nationality policy while preserving the territorial integrity and ethnoterritorial structure of the remainder of the Soviet Union were such that many Soviet as well as Western analysts became pessimistic about the chances for success.[21] Given the glaring disparities in economic, social, and cultural development, the demands of major ethnic groups were often irreconcilable. Under such conditions, only a strong central state with massive resources at its disposal, operating a redistributive economy with the help of an extensive coercive apparatus, could preserve internal stability. Yet even these conditions no longer obtained in the Soviet Union, nor could they have been recreated.

As Suny argues, the struggle in the Soviet Union was not one between the forces of democracy and the forces of empire, but between the conceptions of nation and empire. The disintegration of this empire presented serious concerns. Separatism may have been the best guarantee for democratization in Lithuania, but this was not so clear in Moldova, Azerbaijan, or Russia itself. The proposal for reform from the "bottom-up" was also problematic. What constituted this "bottom" – the union republics, the autonomous republics, or individual ethnic groups? Who could be considered a legitimate representative of each sub-federal unit? It was feared that ethnic formations formerly subservient to Moscow could become new regional hegemons, and might come into conflict with national minorities within their own borders.

On the other hand, those who supported the continuation of the empire had trouble drawing on the popular support of Russians. Public opinion surveys indicated that support for the preservation of the Soviet Union was limited and declining in the Russian Republic (RSFSR). A survey conducted by the All-Union Center on Public Opinion Studies on March 9, 1991 found that 65 percent of those polled thought that the union represented shortages, lines, and poverty, 28 percent felt that it represented arbitrariness and humiliation, 25 percent stated that it would guarantee peace, and only 3 percent said that it gave them a sense of pride in their "socialist fatherland."[22] The most striking result of the March 1991 referendum on the preservation of the union was the disparity between Russian support for the referendum and the support of the rest of the republics. Between 90 and 95 percent of the eligible voters in the Central Asian republics were in favor of the preservation of the USSR, while only 53.5 percent of Russians voted for the union. The low vote in favor was in spite of a massive campaign by the Soviet mass media urging voters to support the union. In addition, most of the support was among the less-educated and rural residents of the republic.[23]

This was a clear indication that the support for a continuation of the union was greatest precisely in those areas where Gorbachev needed it the least. In 1991, the accelerating deterioration of Soviet economic performance, the sharp polarization between reformist and conservative forces in the all-Union government, the growing political role of the republican governments (with the particular strengthening of the position of the separatist republics), and the results of the referendum on the preservation of the Soviet Union led to a shift in Gorbachev's approach to the national question. Faced with the choice between the hard-liners' pressure to maintain the Soviet Union through force by imposing a new Union Treaty from above and the democratic demand to concede real sovereignty to the republics, Gorbachev struck a deal with Yeltsin and the leaders of those nine republics which participated in the March 1991 referendum.

In 1991, Yeltsin expressed confidence that the republics would be able to reach a new Union Treaty "not because they are compelled to do this, but because their wish to live together corresponds to their interests."[24] But the transition from a state-centered to a market economy is a long and protracted process, and the smaller separatist republics believed that marketizing reforms would best be undertaken by their own national governments. In fact, the Union Treaty that was taking shape in the summer of 1991 would have encouraged this approach to reform.

Anti-reformist officials in the central government, believing that the new treaty would lead to the collapse of the political system, engaged in an ill-conceived seizure of the central apparatus in August. The plotters, led in name by Vice-President Gennadi Yanayev, represented the most conservative elements of a dying political order. It was of some importance that the coup received only tentative support within this apparatus itself, with many officials engaging in passive or active resistance to the new leadership. Yet the coup attempt, and its failure, also decisively demonstrated that no problem plaguing the Soviet system, economic or otherwise, could be divorced from the nationality issue. Republican leaders such as Yeltsin and Kirghiz President Askar Akaev became the primary targets of the so-called "Committee of Eight," with Soviet military helicopters reportedly flying over Akaev's residence. In turn, the primary opposition to the coup was regionally based, even if this opposition was not quite universal in scope.

The barricades surrounding the Russian Parliament building during the coup are the most enduring image of opposition to the old order. The building became a powerful symbol of resistance that the plotters themselves were unwilling or unable to confront directly. Russian leaders engaged in active consultations with military, political, and economic officials, and maintained continuous contact with the international community. A relatively small number of military defections served to illustrate the willingness to defend Russian sovereignty physically – indeed, members of Parliament reportedly carried small arms inside the building. It is striking that after the coup attempt, Yeltsin emerged as the predominant political figure – not (as one might have expected in different circumstances) a coalition of opposition military officers or other officials.

Less well known than Russian defiance are the reactions by other regions to the coup. The Baltic states strongly resisted the coup, facing down the attempts by regional officials such as Latvian Communist Party First Secretary, Alfreds Rubiks, to seize power. Moldovan President Mircea Snegur condemned the coup attempt and supported Yeltsin, banning any publications by central press organs such as *Pravda* and setting up a Supreme Security Council in order to organize resistance to the Committee. Akaev strongly asserted his republic's independence and fired the Kirghiz KGB chief, appealing to the UN for assistance and banning all Communist Party activity in the republic. Ukrainian President Leonid Kravchuk, facing reports that Soviet troops were active in the republic, denounced any "anti-constitutional" measures that the coup leaders might undertake, called for calm in Ukrainian territory, and demanded Gorbachev's release and the convocation of an extraordinary meeting of the Supreme Soviet. The Armenian Supreme Soviet rejected the authority of the coup leaders, although President Levon Ter-Petrosyan called for calm and stability in the republic (instead of active resistance) and claimed that he was in direct contact with the all-Union leadership. Georgian President Zviad Gamsakhurdia also called for calm, but used the coup to justify a sweeping purge of his government, removing his Prime Minister, Tengiz Sigua, and his Foreign Minister, Georgi Khoshtaria. On August 22, Radio Tbilisi began to broadcast in the Georgian language.

Other republican leaders were either supportive of the coup, or noncommittal in their response. In Tajikistan, President Kakhar Makhmanov reportedly supported the leaders, allowing the resolutions by the committee to be printed in the republic. Azerbaijan's Ayaz Mutalibov would later deny that he supported the coup (although he supported the committee's call to disarm illegal formations), but according to some accounts he was in favor of the removal of Gorbachev and was prepared to instigate a crackdown in the republic. There were also reports that pictures of Gorbachev had been removed from government buildings in the republic. Uzbek President Islam Karimov supported the State Committee for the State of Emergency, and strongly criticized the policies associated with perestroika. After the coup, Karimov maintained a strong hold in his republic, banning the activities of significant social movements such as the Islamic Renaissance Party. Even Kazakh President Nursultan Nazarbayev, a vocal critic of the coup who resigned from the Politburo in its aftermath and who refused to impose a state of emergency in his republic, combined his denunciations of the coup with criticism of Gorbachev and a call for new elections for the Soviet presidency.

Some ethnic groups within the republics, particularly minorities and Russian settler communities, supported the activities of the committee. This became a significant controversy in Moldova after the coup attempt, when Moldovan officials arrested two Gagauz leaders, Stepan Topal and Mikhail Kendigelyan, and the Dniester Russian leader, Igor Smirnov. The arrests led to huge demonstrations, with many Russians in Moldova expressing their desire to secede from the republic or to move individually to the Russian Federation. Russian officials were called in to mediate the conflict, much as they had (with some initial success) in the Armenia–Azerbaijan conflict over Nagorno-Karabakh.

Ultimately, the coup attempt accelerated processes that were already underway in the Soviet Union. The Baltic states and Ukraine achieved independence, and all republics gained more sovereignty over their own affairs. Gorbachev and Yeltsin found themselves mutually dependent, Gorbachev dependent on the Russian leadership to finance a mushrooming deficit and Yeltsin using a weakened and discredited center buffer to alleviate the fears of others of Russian hegemony. Bilateral and multilateral negotiations between regional leaders after the coup tended to focus on the economic and military dimension of their interdependence, in some cases bypassing the center altogether. But the secession of Ukraine in December 1991 effectively dashed all remaining prospects for preserving even a loosely confederated union, leaving open the question of what economic, military, and political agreements might be reached among the parts of the former union, and indeed whether any such arguments were likely to be implemented.

Implications for Western policy

As James Mayall argues, "the three great waves of modern state creation – in Latin America in the nineteenth century, in Europe after 1919, and Asia, Africa, the Caribbean and the Pacific after 1945 – have all been associated with the collapse of empires."[25] The collapse of the Soviet empire has raised significant questions about the stance which the West should take towards the emergence of a new state system in the present territory of the Soviet Union. In the United States, two opposing positions emerged, with some analysts and politicians calling for policies actively promoting Soviet disintegration and others advocating policies designed to bolster the Soviet central government and preserving the integrity of the USSR.[26] By the early 1990s, however, it had become increasingly clear that the major problem for both the Soviet population and the international community involved not so much the preservation or disintegration of the Soviet Union, but rather the nature of the changes which would take place in its territory. As Alexei Arbatov lucidly argued, the dangers posed by disintegration were not so pressing as Westerners frequently believed, and those in the Soviet administration and the military who kept "blackmailing the West and the Soviet people alike by doomsday prophecies of chaos and civil war" were primarily interested in preserving their dominant positions in the centralized Soviet regime.[27]

The international community could play only a limited role in facilitating or preventing Soviet disintegration in any case. The breakdown of the Soviet infrastructure and the upsurge of nationalism in the Soviet Union could not be reversed by a simple infusion of capital or by the signing of nuclear arms reductions treaties. Further arms agreements might have reduced the number of weapons in the hands of future leaders, and thereby contributed to greater security, but would have done little to strengthen the center. Furthermore, there was no coherently articulated vision by external actors (including the USA) as to what the future shape of the Soviet Union should have been, other than the fact that the system should aim at embracing liberal economic principles. The enthusiastic support for the Soviet center did wane by late 1991, but there remained real ambivalence about embracing republican leaders such as Yeltsin or Georgia's Gamsakhurdia.

Western programs of economic aid may play a significant role over the long term, but should be crafted with some care. Such policies can no longer presume the economic unity and territorial integrity of the old union, but will have to be tailored to the distinctive problems facing specific territorial markets. Moreover, because the number of primary actors in the international system has multiplied, and the USA is no longer the central economic hegemon, coordinating policy towards this region will be a major challenge for the West.

When analyzing alternatives for the future development of the new states, a number of considerations about the links connecting nationalism, markets, and democracy should be taken into account. It has already been argued that the goals of making a successful transition to a market economy and of preserving the old imperial order are mutually incompatible. The former Soviet republics find themselves at very different stages of social and economic development. A highly repressive political regime would be required to keep together regions as different as the Baltic states and Central Asia, which are characterized by an enormous and growing gulf in their economic, political, and demographic behavior and in their industrial and political culture. The human and material resources needed to maintain such a regime have by and large been exhausted. Whether even a loose economic federation – a common market or commonwealth – is now viable is in question.

As the experience of the economic blockade of Lithuania or that of the military crackdown on the governments of Lithuania and Latvia in 1991 has demonstrated, attempts to keep the secessionist-minded republics within the Soviet Union strengthened existing antimarket and antidemocratic structures, waste the resources which could have been better utilized for economic reforms, and placed further strains on the relationship with the West.

In a recently published book Eric Hobsbawm argues that "the characteristic nationalist movements of the late 20th century are essentially negative, or rather divisive" and do not provide an alternative principle for the political restructuring of the world in the twenty-first century.[28] The present evolution of Soviet-type societies demonstrates that this type of approach towards nationalism and secessionism in the Soviet Union and Eastern Europe needs to be fundamentally reconsidered. The Soviet experience should serve as a reminder that the nexus between nationalism, marketization and a liberal democratic world order is much stronger than liberal and Marxist critics of nationalism will admit.

Leaders of a number of former Soviet republics rightly believe that their separation from the Soviet Union and their integration into the world market and new international order are one and the same thing.[29] The Baltic states and Ukraine seek incorporation into other supranational communities, like the European Free Trade Association, the emerging Baltic Commonwealth, or the European Community. The Central Asian states seek greater integration with the developing economies of Asia. It is already evident that the Baltic states have not pursued autarkic policies with regard to the non-Baltic states – Lithuania has entered into independent trade agreements with both Ukraine and Russia.

Both the nationalist idea and the international system have undergone a major evolution in the course of this century. An international order capable of condemning the irrational and destructive potential of xenophobic forms of nationalism, and major violations of human rights and ecological standards, has by and large been created. Regional leaders in the former Soviet Union have clearly been influenced by these international norms in drafting their programs for reform and in seeking membership in international organizations. In these conditions, the national movements in the Soviet Union are not uniformly "essentially negative or rather divisive." On the contrary, the breakup of the Soviet Union may represent a real precondition for greater global cooperation on social, economic, and ecological issues.

NOTES

1 See Richard Pipes, *The Formation of the Soviet Union: Communism and Nationalism, 1917–1923* (Cambridge, MA: Harvard University Press, 1954) and Gerhard Simon, *Nationalism and Policy Toward the Nationalities in the Soviet Union* (Boulder: Westview, 1991).
2 Despite our use of the term "empire" in this introduction, it is important to note that the Soviet Union is fundamentally distinct from other historical empires, such as the Habsburg or Ottoman empires. The Soviet Union had a unique territorial base, with a political system which only indirectly reflected the interests of the dominant nationality (and which has frequently worked against those interests). While the center clearly exercised political control over the periphery, the redistributive and non-market aspects of the state-controlled economy had little in common with the classic imperial model.
3 See Gregory J. Massell, "Modernization and National Policy in Soviet Central Asia: Problems and Prospects," in Paul Cocks, Robert V. Daniels, and Nancy Whittier Heer, eds., *Dynamics of Soviet Politics* (Cambridge MA: Harvard University Press, 1976), pp. 265–290.
4 Ernest Gellner, "Nationalism and the Two Forms of Cohesion in Complex Societies," in Ernest Gellner, *Culture, Identity, and Politics* (Cambridge University Press, 1987), pp. 26–27.
5 Leokadia M. Drobizheva, *Dukhovnaia obshchnost' narodov SSSR* (Moscow: 1981); Fred Grupp and Ellen Jones, "Modernization and Ethnic Equalization in the USSR," *Soviet Studies*, 36:2, 1984.
6 Yuri Ginter and Mikk Titma, "Sravnitel'nyi analiz razvitiia soiuznykh respublik," *Sotsiologicheskie issledovaniia*, 6, 1987.
7 Edward Allworth, "The New Central Asians," in Edward Allworth (ed.), *Central Asia. 120 Years of Russian Rule* (Durham, NC: Duke University Press, 1989), p. 572.
8 Ernest Gellner, *Nations and Nationalism* (Ithaca, NY: Cornell University Press, 1983); Miroslav Hroch, "How Much Does Nation Formation Depend on Nationalism?" *East European Politics and Societies*, 4: 1, Winter 1990.

9 See Sophie Quinn-Judge, "Parting of the Ways," *Far Eastern Economic Review*, October 3, 1991, pp. 16–18.

10 *Journal of Soviet Nationalities*, 1: 2, 1990, p. 171.

11 Aleksandr Solzhenitsyn, "Kak nam obustroit' Rossiiu," *Literaturnaia gazeta*, September 18, 1990, pp. 3–6.

12 Its propensity to strike an alliance with anti-Western forces in the Third World was demonstrated during the Gulf crisis, when a number of right-wing Russian nationalists openly called for support of Hussein's regime in Iraq.

13 Gavriil Popov, "Za chto golosuet Rossiia," *Ogonek*, 10, 1990, p. 6.

14 See Joseph C. Brandt, "Economic Reform and the Soviet National Question," *Telos*, 84, Summer 1990; *Izvestiia*, February 6–7, 1991.

15 Philip Goldman, "*Perestroika*: End or Beginning of Soviet Federalism?" *Telos*, 84, Summer 1990. Indeed, the 1989 Platform represented the peak of Gorbachev's liberalism and spelled out the maximum concessions to the republics that could be made short of granting political independence; the leadership's later policies actually retreated from that framework until the 1991 Union Treaty.

16 Quoted in *Report on the USSR*, 1: 39, 1989, p. 2.

17 "Natsional'naia politika partii v sovremennykh usloviiakh. Platforma KPSS," *Pravda*, September 24, 1989, p. 1.

18 *Ibid.*

19 Quoted in *Daily Report: Soviet Union*, January 15, 1991, p. 41.

20 "Finding Ways to Renew Party Work," *Pravda*, January 11, 1991, p. 2, in *Daily Report: Soviet Union*, January 17, 1991, p. 32.

21 Zbigniew Brzezinski, "Brzezinski on the Breakup of the USSR," *World Monitor*, November 1990, pp. 30–33; Valerii Tishkov, "My propustili XX vek ..." in *Perestroika i national'nye problemy. Prilozhenie k zhurnalu Novoe vremia*, December 1989, pp. 4–6.

22 *RFE/RL Daily Report* (49), March 11, 1991.

23 *Pravda*, March 22, 1991, p. 1; Ann Sheehy, "USSR – The All-Union and RSFSR Referendum of March 17: Results," *RFE/RL*, March 26, 1991.

24 Quoted in Serge Schmemann, "Yeltsin Attains Greater Powers in his Republic", *The New York Times*, April 6, 1991, p. 1.

25 James Mayall, *Nationalism and International Society*, Cambridge Studies in International Relations, no. 10 (Cambridge University Press, 1990), p. 156.

26 The two opposite approaches can be found in William Safire, "Landsbergis for Nobel Laureate," *The New York Times*, May 9, 1991, p. A19, and in Christopher Layne's recent article "America's Stake in Soviet Stability", *World Policy Journal*, Winter 1990–1991, 8: 1, pp. 61–88.

27 Alexei Arbatov, "Rearranging the Order Falling Apart: Prospects and Alternatives for European Security," Paper presented at the conference on "The Future of European Security", April 24–25, 1991, University of California, Berkeley.

28 Eric Hobsbawm, *Nations and Nationalism Since 1780: Programme, Myth, Reality* (Cambridge University Press, 1990), pp. 164 and 173.

29 Victor Zaslavsky, "Soviet Transition to a Market Economy: State Dependent Workers, Populism, and Nationalism," forthcoming.

2 State, civil society, and ethnic cultural consolidation in the USSR – roots of the national question

RONALD SUNY

The explosions of ethnic nationalism and separatism in Gorbachev's Soviet Union seem to confirm the metaphor of empire as appropriate to the Soviet regime. A century and a half ago the European traveller, the Marquis de Custine, called the tsarist empire "the prison house of nations," and that term has enjoyed a long run as a description of the imperialism of tsardom's Soviet successor. The Soviet slogans that masked ethnic tensions and inequalities, the rhetoric of internationalism and *druzhba narodov*, have been overwhelmed by the rainbow of national flags that proclaim the self-assertion of peoples whose identities had long been contained within prescribed formulae. Nations have emerged within the empire, and in that emergence the empire has begun to die. After the coup in August 1991, it appears unlikely that it will miraculously spring back to life, or in its death agony transform itself into a new democratic multinational state. But what supra-state formation may emerge in the new constellation of "independent" states is, of course, one of the key political questions of our time.

Conventionally empire is understood to be a large state made up of many peoples or nationalities, ruled by a central power that usually represents one people holding a privileged position in the political and social hierarchy of the empire.[1] Thus, empire is inherently an inequitable political arrangement, a relationship of subordination and superordination, hierarchical and usually exploitative of the subordinate ethnicities. Since few peoples willingly accept a subordinate role as exploited subject, at least in the age of nationalism and democracy, the imperial relationship is one that is ultimately maintained more by force and violence than by consensus. Given freedom of choice, subject nationalities would opt for either equality within the reformed state, a degree of autonomy based on ethnicity, or separation and independence. In this way a multinational state is pulled between imperial, centralizing tendencies and disintegrating ones that include self-expression, autonomy, equality, and sovereignty.

Empire is understandably contrasted to nation, and the two often are seen as mutually exclusive, subversive to one another, as in the Habsburg or Ottoman empires where the rise of nationalism and the formation of ethnic nations undermined the imperial, dynastic principles on which the multinational empires had been built. But equally threatening to empire is democracy, the legally guaranteed popular participation in the choosing of government. The more democratic a state becomes, the less it can maintain inequitable imperial relationships. A truly democratic state would involve not only majority rule, but legal protection for the rights of minorities.

If one accepts these introductory notions, it appears that the Soviet Union moved in the late 1980s and early 1990s – and indeed even before then – from a centralized, Russian-dominated empire toward a more decentralized multinational state with more democratic features. Not only within the state but in its inter-state relations with the formerly subordinate states of east Central Europe, Moscow under Gorbachev has gradually been surrendering its former position of dominance and exploitation. But as relatively peaceful as the transformation of inter-state relations in Eastern Europe has been to date (with the notable exception of Romania), the parallel metamorphosis within the Soviet Union was marked by inter-ethnic violence, an explosion of national chauvinism and anti-Semitism, and a desperate drive by several Soviet republics toward national independence, no matter what the consequence for Gorbachev, his program of perestroika, and the Soviet Union they wished to leave behind.

In the rush to understand the cascade of events that threatened the Soviet Union, little attention has been paid to the long-term causes of the swelling wave of nationalism in the Soviet Union. In a most interesting article on "Post-Communist Nationalism," published in *Foreign Affairs*, one of the classic theorists of totalitarianism, Zbigniew Brzezinski, argued that "communism in fact intensified popular nationalist passions." Though in the current daily barrage of news of nationalist expression in the Soviet Union, such an announcement may not seem startling, it in fact marked a reversal of a long and powerful tradition in sovietological thought. For the original model of totalitarianism, so influential during the long years of the Cold War consensus, not so much denied the relevance of nationality, ethnicity, or nationalism in discussing the Soviet Union as it simply did not notice the multinational potential for resistance. When Brzezinski and Friedrich listed the "islands of separateness" that potentially offered some resistance to totalitarian rule, they mentioned family, churches, universities, writers, and artists, but not nationalities. Indeed, for much of the last four decades the study of nationality has been marginalized in Soviet studies, the appropriate field for discontented émigrés nostalgic for a lost homeland, bitter over the conquest by communists. The mainstream of the profession dealt with the USSR as if it were monolithic, not only politically and socially, but ethnically as well.

Even in his reassessment of the course of Soviet history Brzezinski brought to his review the kind of top-down approach, beginning with politics and ideology, that was so characteristic of the totalitarian school of thinking. In Brzezinski's view Gorbachev's decentralization "created an opportunity for long-suppressed national grievances to surface." Popular nationalism is the national response to communist oppression:

... communism in fact intensified popular nationalist passions. It produced a political culture imbued with intolerance, self-righteousness, rejection of social compromise and a massive inclination toward self-glorifying oversimplification. On the level of belief, dogmatic communism thus fused with and even reinforced intolerant nationalism; on the level of practice, the destruction of such relatively internationalist social classes as the aristocracy or the business elite further reinforced the populist inclination toward nationalistic chauvinism. Nationalism was thereby nurtured, rather than diluted in the communist experience.[2]

Without question the real historic experience of the non-Russian peoples in the Soviet Union shaped the present forms of action and discourse in which they are engaged.

But the actual generation of the centrifugal nationalisms of the Soviet peoples, including that of the Great Russians, is not so easily explained as the result of natural impulses long suppressed and released by a new dawn of relative freedom. In place of what might be called the "sleeping beauty" approach to nationalism – nationalism as the essential and authentic expression of ethnic communities – I would like to suggest what I want to call the "making of nations" approach. This is the idea that nationality as well as nationalism, like other social and cultural formations, is the product of real historical conjunctures in which ethnic communities, activist intelligentsias, and political imperatives have worked together to create a new level of national coherence, consolidation, and consciousness. One of the central ironies of Soviet history is that a regime dedicated to effacing nationality and to creating a supra-ethnic community and a party that posited that class rather than nationality was the key determinant of social structure have presided over a process in which modern nations have been formed within the union they governed. These Soviet nations, though built on earlier ethnic communities and elite nationalist movements, are largely the result of the complex history of the seventy years after the Russian Revolution.

Before and during the revolution Russian imperial rule over the non-Russian peoples was quite inconsistent and had an extraordinarily varied effect on the tsar's subjects. The tsarist state promoted certain peoples in the empire at some times (for example, the Baltic Germans and the Armenian merchants until the 1880s) and discriminated against others (Jews, Ukrainians, and Poles particularly after 1863, Armenians after 1885, and Finns at the turn of the century). After 1881 the ruling nationality, the Russians, increasingly conceived of social problems in ethnic terms and saw Jewish conspiracies, Armenian separatists, and nationalists in general as sources of disruption and rebellion. Such enmity and discrimination directed against whole peoples, regardless of social status, helped erase internal distinctions of members of the ethnic group under attack and engendered support for the conceptions of the nationalists. Yet even as the nationalist construction of the ethnic enemy gained in power, the economic developmental policies of tsarism and considerations of security and profit attracted certain national bourgeoisies to try to work with the Russifying regime. Moreover, the embryonic working classes of Russia's peripheries remained ambivalent about nationalism in most cases and expressed their ethnic consciousness obliquely through ethnic socialist movements.

As the seigniorial economy gave way to market relations, and new forms of the exploitation of labor replaced more traditional-sanctioned and paternalistic ones, those peoples that more immediately experienced industry and city life were recruited by radical intellectuals for socialist movements, but the degree and the nature of their mobilization was affected by their ethnic as well as class sense of oppression. At particular conjunctures, ethnicity and class reinforced one another, and at other times undermined each other. In central Transcaucasia, Georgian nobles and peasants, sharing a common ethnic culture and values based on rural, pre-capitalist traditions, faced an entrepreneurial Armenian urban middle class that dominated their historic capital, Tiflis, and that had developed a way of life alien to the villagers. To the east, in and around Baku, the peasantry was almost entirely Azerbaijani, and urban society was stratified roughly along ethnic and religious lines, with Muslim workers at the bottom, Armenian and Russian workers in the more skilled positions, and Christian and European industrialists and capitalists dominating the oil industry.[3] At the same time, the vertical ethnic ties that linked different social strata or classes together in a single community worked against the horizontal links between members of the same social class.[4]

Like socialism, nationalism in tsarist Russia was largely an urban phenomenon, and no matter how sincerely patriots may have extolled the virtues of the peasantry, making actual converts among villagers proved to be as difficult for the followers of Shevchenko as for the disciples of Marx. Yet even though most of the non-Russian peoples of the tsarist empire were overwhelmingly peasant, their radically differ-ent historic experiences and positions were matched by differences in degree of national consciousness. Some peoples, like the Belorussians, Lithuanians, and Azerbaijanis, were distinguished by their almost completely peasant composition and low level of national conscious-ness. In contrast, the Ukrainians and Estonians were marked by social and geographic divisions and a profound ambiguity in their national and class orientations. Yet a third group – Georgians and Latvians – resolved the tension between nationality and class through a socialist-oriented national movement. The fourth – the Finns – divided radi-cally into fiercely opposing camps, one socialist, the other nationalist, that resolved their conflict through bloody repression. And, finally, the Armenians subordinated class divisions to a vertically integrating nationalism.

The development of ethnic cohesion and national awareness – not to mention political nationalism – was related to the effects on various peoples of the general socio-economic transformation that took place in Russia in the decades following the Emancipation of 1861. Some peoples continued to have little representation in towns (for example, Lithuanians, Ukrainians, and Belorussians) or, if they did migrate to industrial or urban centers, tended to assimilate into the predomin-antly Russian work force. Their experience differed radically from those ethnicities who developed a working class of their own (Georg-ians, Latvians, Estonians, Jews, and to an extent, Armenians), who experienced industrial capitalism more directly, and came into contact with the radical intelligentsia. Yet a third group, which included most of the Muslim peoples of the empire, had little contact with the social revolution of industrialism, relatively little urban experience, and less contact with the socialist or nationalist intelligentsia. (Here one should be careful to differentiate between Muslim peoples, some of whom, like the Azerbaijanis and the Volga Tatars, had a significant if small urban presence.)

During the first year of the revolution hopes for a constitutional solution to the problem of multinationality moderated the demands of the nationalists, and social concerns were far more widely articulated than ethnic ones. But after the October Revolution, in a period of economic collapse and the disintegration of state power, with the rise of a domestic armed opposition to Bolshevism and the intervention of foreign armies, a more vociferous nationalism rose among many non-Russian peoples. In part, this was due to the spread of the revolution outside urban centers into the countryside where the non-Russian majorities lived. Lines of conflict were drawn up that emphasized ethnicity (Russian workers against Ukrainian peasants, Armenian bourgeoisie against Georgian workers and peasants). In part, it was the product of the hostility felt by nationalist intellectuals to the ostensibly internationalist, but evidently Russocentric, Bolsheviks; and in part, it was a phenomenon encouraged and financed by the interventionists. In any case, the rise of nationalism in the Russian Civil War was no more the natural outcome of an inevitable historical process, the inherent and organic working out of the "natural" aspirations of the minorities, than was the rise of class consciousness during the first year of revolution the inevitable maturing of inarticulate proletarians. Both the development of class consciousness in the cities in 1917 and the subsequent spread of nationalism beyond the intelligentsia were products of long-term social, cultural, and intellectual processes that began in the nineteenth century and of more immediate experiences of the revolutionary years.

Because fifty or sixty years later, after decades of Soviet or independent development, many of the incipient nations of 1917 forged national-cultural identities, established state structures, and manifested political nationalism, in retrospective histories the revolutionary years are viewed as if that future had already existed in 1917. The nationalist representation of an essential, if concealed, national consciousness, ever present and emerging when opportunity knocked, seemed borne out by subsequent events and therefore was read back into an earlier age. My argument, however, is that much of the story of nation-building, and even nationality formation, for many peoples of the Russian empire belongs more appropriately in the Soviet period than in the years before the Civil War.[5]

Before the revolutions of 1917 most of the constituent peoples of what later made up the Soviet Union were not yet fully formed, self-conscious nations. Though ethno-linguistic communities with distinct religious and ethnic cultures had existed since prehistoric times on what became Soviet territory, few of the peoples of the Russian empire had coalesced around the more modern notions of a secular, territorial nation. Most had never had a state in the past, and nationalist ideas expressed by urban intellectuals had not yet spread to the less educated, either in towns or the countryside. Even during the years of revolution and Civil War (1917–1921), when independent and semi-independent national states appeared on the borders of ethnic Russia, nationalism was still largely a phenomenon centered around educated townspeople, students, and the lower middle classes, with only an unstable following in the countryside.

With the end of the Civil War several major nationalities found themselves independent of the Soviet Union. As a result of Soviet weakness, effective resistance to native Bolshevik adherents, and Western intervention, the Poles, Finns, Lithuanians, Estonians, and Latvians created their own independent states. Those left under Soviet rule – Russians, Ukrainians, Belorussians, Moldavians, Armenians, Georgians, Azerbaijanis, and other Muslim peoples – were organized in a new federal state, the first ever to base its political units on ethnicity. Marxist theory at the time proposed that nationalism and national exclusivity could eventually be eliminated through the real development of socialism, but even this simplistic reduction of ethnic culture and national formation to the economic base recognized the contemporary power of the appeal of nationality. Consistently a defender of "national self-determination," Lenin proposed a post-revolutionary compromise: to maximize national political and cultural autonomy within a federation dominated by the Communist Party and to condemn the over-centralizing tendencies of more Russian chauvinist members of the Party (among whom he included Stalin).[6] Committed ideologically to Lenin's idea of national self-determination (to the point of separation!), the Bolsheviks at the same time believed that Soviet power was an historically advanced stage beyond parliamentary democracy and that the rule of the working class through its vanguard, the Communist Party, was a sufficient guarantee of the interests of the population as a whole. The Soviet Union had been formed in the Civil War by the victories of the Red Army and the defeats of the ethnic nationalists. The rhetoric of internationalism and the federalism of the new state ultimately did not prevent the rapid establishment of inequitable, hierarchical, imperial relationships between the center and the peripheral peoples. Power rather than persuasion was the final arbiter.

Although the republics quickly lost real state sovereignty, each nationality maintained its own republic or autonomous district in which the national language and culture were to be encouraged and where native cadres were to dominate in administration. This policy of "nativization" (*korenizatsiia*), encouraged by Lenin (and even supported by Stalin for a time), was sincerely carried out in the 1920s with spectacular results. The ethnic republics became demographically and culturally more ethnic. In Ukraine, as in other republics, a cultural renaissance blossomed. Russians seeking higher education there had to learn in Ukrainian.[7] Many smaller peoples who had never had a written language were provided with alphabets, and campaigns for literacy promoted both socialism and national culture simultaneously. Even the Jews, who did not have a republic of their own, benefitted from this policy, enjoying a revival of Yiddish learning and culture, the formation of a Jewish section of the Communist Party, and a new security from a state that legislated against manifestations of anti-Semitism.[8] At the same time, however, the Bolshevik program of modernization had a more ambivalent effect on the nationalities, simultaneously undermining various traditions and cultural institutions, often brutally attacking the Church, campaigning against patriarchy, and subverting traditional patterns of leadership and deference. Furthermore, the shift from village to town, farm to factory, gave millions of ethnic peasants greater social mobility, higher education, and broader cultural and intellectual horizons. The legacy of October for millions of Soviet citizens, regardless of their ethnicity, was upward mobility, access to education, and the promise of material improvement.[9]

By the early 1930s, once Stalin had consolidated the hegemony of his faction within the Party, the imperatives of rapid industrialization and the massive effort of forcing peasants into collective farms carried the Party leadership toward a more expedient nationality policy. Nativization as a deliberate state policy almost immediately suffered from the Stalin revolution of the 1930s and the revival under his personal autocracy of Russian chauvinism. Stalin had never reconciled himself to Lenin's notion of federalism, and though he preserved the form he created a unitary state, highly centralized, with little political autonomy left to the peripheries. Through the instrument of police terror he destroyed the last vestiges of "national Communism," imprisoning or executing tens of thousands of ethnic Communist leaders in the Great Purges. All hints of small-nation nationalism were severely punished, and Russian culture was promoted as the most advanced in the USSR. At the end of the 1930s, study of the Russian language was made compulsory in all schools – though the non-Russian languages continued to be taught in the ethnic areas. Industrialization led to the migration of hundreds of thousands of Russians and other Slavs to Central Asia and (after their annexation to the Soviet Union in the early 1940s) to the Baltic republics. Even when some accommodation was made to national and religious feeling, as during the struggle against the Nazis in World War II, the new emphasis on Russian patriotic themes and national heroes subordinated the non-Russian peoples to the state's primary efforts to defend and develop the country economically. Several small peoples – the Crimean Tatars, Meskhetian Turks, Volga Germans, Karachai, Kalmyks, Balkars, Ingush, and Chechens – were condemned as traitors to the Soviet state and forcibly removed from their homelands and sent into Central Asian exile.[10] During the years of Stalinism the Soviet Union most closely resembled the ideal type of an empire – centralized, ruled by force and a unitary ideology, with the dominant nationality, the Russians, gaining a distinctly superior position in the state and in public perception.

Nevertheless, despite the political repression of the Stalin years and the abandonment of much of the cultural program of *korenizatsiia*, the non-Russians managed to maintain their demographic and cultural hold on several of the republics. By the time of Stalin's death the so-called titular nationalities dominated in numbers in most of the republics, even though they had been unable to establish any real political autonomy or carry on any nationalist expression for nearly a quarter of a century.[11] When the worst excesses of Stalinism were eliminated by Khrushchev in the early 1950s, tentative national expression reappeared – first in the form of reprinted writers, rehabilitated victims of the *Stalinshchina*, and new themes in art, film, and literature. A part of the national heritage of non-Russians was officially sanctioned, promoted, and, in a sense, appropriated as part of the collective Soviet past. At the same time significant historical figures, even whole movements central to historical understanding, were beyond the newly established limits of discussion. Armenian Dashnaks, Georgian Mensheviks, nationalist poets, or those who had fled abroad were ritualistically condemned by officialdom. Yet in the atmosphere of increased freedom the border between the forbidden and the acceptable was constantly crossed by emboldened writers and principled dissidents.

Khrushchev also established a more decentralized political and economic system, though this limited political autonomy was far from democratic. With less control from the center, but in the absence of any real democracy, limited political autonomy resulted in the strengthening of local elites, most of them carryovers from Stalin's time. In Transcaucasia and Central Asia particularly, local ethnic "mafias" gained control of the economy and political patronage systems. Corruption, bribery, and the advancement of friends or relatives into positions of power became the norm for local administrators. As long as the Communist leaders in the republics could placate Moscow by maintaining stability, keeping some restraints on nationalism, and showing economic growth, they remained relatively free from reprisals from the center. The perverse result of the end of terror and centralization was the strengthening of already powerful ethno-political machines that ripped off the state economic sector, patronized the "second economy," and satisfied significant parts of the local population who either benefitted from the spoils system or enjoyed the usually freer way of life in their homelands. "Diamond" Anton Kochinian, First Secretary of the Communist Party in Armenia, and the rapacious Vasilii Mzhavanadze, his counterpart in Georgia, were matched in their venality and brazen disregard of the law by petty party potentates in Central Asia, most notoriously Uzbekistan's Sharaf Rashidov.

For nearly a decade after the fall of Khrushchev in 1964, little changed for the national elites. The conservative cadre policy of "chairman of the board," Leonid Brezhnev, encouraged the corruption until it enveloped all parts of the Soviet Union and reached into the family of Brezhnev himself. No attempt was made at structural reform, however. The problem of the non-Russian regions was dealt with administratively and only very rarely by changes of the top leadership. In Central Asia and the Baltic republics, party chiefs stayed in power for decades.[12] In Transcaucasia, where the "second economy" had grown to gargantuan proportions by the early 1970s and economic indicators dipped ever lower, attempts were made to bring in personnel from outside the patronage system. In 1969 Heidar Aliev, a career KGB officer, was named first secretary of the Azerbaijani Communist Party. Three years later Eduard Shevardnadze, also from the security apparatus, became head of the Georgian party, and in 1974 Karen Demirjian, an engineer educated outside of Armenia, was brought in to head the Armenian party. Their mandates were similar: to end the corruption and system of favoritism in personnel decisions, to contain the growing nationalism, and stimulate the local economies. Success was mixed. Purges of thousands of officials only temporarily affected "business as usual." The "second economy" was too deeply imbedded in kinship networks and local cultural prohibitions against betrayal of friends, patrons, and clients to be eradicated or even seriously injured by changes at the top.[13] As Brezhnev, ever more feeble, clung to power, the local "mafias" held sway in the border republics and former reformers, like Aliev and Demirjian, became the beneficiaries of their own power networks. Cynicism, disillusionment, and a growing pessimism marked the dominant mood in the population. Economic and political stagnation eroded the last vestiges of faith in socialism. Some gave up on the Soviet Union altogether and sought refuge abroad. Many retreated into the details of daily life. And still others turned away from the mundane burdens of a spiritless modernization towards nationalism as an internal refuge.

The uneven and contradictory development of nations in the Soviet Union – at the same time consolidating ethnically in some republics while threatened by assimilation, in-migration, and linguistic Russification elsewhere – gave rise to a variety of nationalist responses in the 1960s and 1970s. Some of the deported peoples who had lost their homelands under Stalin, most courageously the Crimean Tatars, organized daring demonstrations in the heart of Moscow. Newly inspired by Israeli military victories and encouraged by supporters abroad, Soviet Jews agitated after 1967 to emigrate to Israel or the West. At first defiantly and later with permission, Armenians marched year after year, beginning in 1965, to commemorate the Genocide of 1915. When in April 1978 the Georgian party tried to remove a clause in the republic's constitution that established Georgian as the official state language, thousands marched to the party headquarters and forced Shevardnadze to reverse the decision. That same year Abkhazians protested against poor treatment by their Georgian overlords and petitioned to join the Russian federated republic. Karabakh Armenians repeatedly raised objections to Azerbaijani restrictions on Armenian culture and learning, but with no results. Ukrainian writers, teachers, and journalists protested against Russian inroads in their republic and suffered a cruel repression. Lithuanians rallied around the Catholic Church, protesting restrictions on religious observance. In Kaunas a student immolated himself by fire. In Muslim Central Asia there was generally little open protest, but many Western observers believed that Islam presented a potential source of cultural resistance to Soviet authority.[14] And perhaps most ominously of all, the same economic, social, and cultural discontents that gave rise to non-Russian nationalisms also affected the Great Russians as well.

Like the national consciousness of smaller nations, that of the Russian was centered on a perception of national danger, of the erosion and irreplaceable loss of culture, of a sense of the past. Like Armenian, Estonian, and other national movements, the Russian was deeply concerned with environmental destruction, with threats to Russian nature, and with the brutal treatment of cultural and religious monuments. This relatively benign affection for the village and the Church was molded by some groups into a vicious xenophobic, anti-Semitic chauvinism that pictured the Russians as a disadvantaged nation victimized by foreigners and the non-Russians of the USSR. Religious nationalists, neo-Slavophiles emphasizing the innate virtues of Slavic peoples, National Bolsheviks combining Russophilia with Great Power chauvinism, and outright fascists emerged on the right wing of underground Russian nationalism in the Brezhnev years, and less virulent versions of their Russocentric ideas could be read in official journals like *Molodaia gvardiia* and *Nash sovremennik*. When a prominent party official (later a close advisor to Gorbachev), Aleksander Yakovlev, strongly criticized the ideology of the nationalists, he was "exiled" to Canada as ambassador. Clearly Russophilia, so alien to Lenin, had deeply penetrated his party in the six decades since his death, and much of the Russian intelligentsia openly admired the sensationalist depictions of tsars and priests of the painter Ilia Glazunov or the religious nationalism, with its explicit authoritarinism, of Aleksander Solzhenitsyn. With the coming of glasnost, the Russian nationalist organization Pamyat (Memory), suspiciously protected by highly placed officials, combined Russophilic themes, a xenophobic sense of national danger, and the now fashionable anti-Stalinism to blame Jews, Latvians, and other non-Russians for the repressions of the Stalinist past and the evident degeneration of Russian life.[15]

The first signs of nationalist resistance to central state policy in the Gorbachev years occurred in December 1986 when the long-serving Kazakh party chief and close friend of the late Leonid Brezhnev, Dinmukhammed Kunaev, was dismissed by Moscow and replaced with a Russian. Young people streamed into the streets in protest at this affront to Kazakh pride and privilege. The protests were condemned, and no concessions were made to the demonstrators. A little over a year later, however, as perestroika and glasnost accelerated, much more sustained and massive nationalist demonstrations were organized by Armenians in Karabakh, an ethnically Armenian enclave within the Azerbaijani republic. Within a few days the gradualistic politics of early perestroika were transformed into the ethno-politics of national self-determination and democratization. In February of 1988, tens of thousands of Armenians marched through the streets of Erevan in support of their compatriots in Mountainous Karabakh in neighboring Azerbaijan, who wished to join their region to the Armenian republic. Even in their defiance the Armenians proclaimed themselves loyal to Soviet power and to the ideals of perestroika. Then, tragically, Azerbaijani youth, incensed at the perceived threat to their republic, went on a rampage in Sumgait in the last days of February, killing their Armenian neighbors indiscriminately.

The events in the Caucasus were followed a few months later by a broad-based, all-class national protest in the Baltic republics over Russian dominance. Demands for greater national autonomy led to the creation of alternative political fronts and to concessions by the Communist parties. While in the Baltic new party leaders found a common language with the nationalists, in Azerbaijan and Armenia martial law and the arrest of the leaders of the protests brought the movements to a temporary halt by the end of 1988. In Moldova, Belorussia, and Ukraine issues from the unburied past, fears about the threat to the native languages, and anxiety about demographic and linguistic Russification brought intellectuals together with their ethnic compatriots in common protests. Peaceful marches, mass meetings, and hunger strikes became daily challenges to the monopoly of power by national Communist parties. In early April 1989 hundreds of demonstrators in Tbilisi were hurt (and at least eighteen killed) when Soviet troops acted swiftly and brutally to quell demands for Georgian independence. Just as each mobilized republic raised its own national flag and resurrected its particular national symbols and myths, so each of these movements developed its own agenda – some were consonant with the plans of the Kremlin reformers, others a deadly challenge to the more tentative process of democratization initiated from the top.

In retrospect it is clear that several new elements had been introduced into Soviet politics in 1988: the public display of "people power"; the reluctance of the Gorbachev government to use armed force against public expressions of nationalism; the eruption of inter-ethnic hostilities that quickly degenerated into pogroms (in Sumgait); and the steady displacement of Communist Party influence by informal nationalist committees and popular fronts. As ethnic expression took bolder form and expanded out from ethnic intellectuals to include broader strata of the population, it metamorphosed into something both deeper and more inclusive than a simple cultural nationalism. Besides the issues of democracy and openness, the Gorbachev initiative had raised questions of the limits of central authority and local autonomy and had given a new political significance to persistent frictions caused by a central state perceived as Russifying. Suddenly, the consequences of attempting to democratize a multinational empire were thrown into high relief. Gorbachev would later admit publicly that "we had underestimated the forces of nationalism and separatism that were hidden deep within our system and their ability to emerge with populist elements creating a socially explosive mixture."[16]

The new mass nationalist movements stemmed from both an increased capacity of ethnic populations to act in their own interest (and not only because of a freer political atmosphere but also because of greater coherence and consciousness of the nationalities themselves) and palpable perceptions of non-Russians (and Russians!) that their nations are in danger, either demographically, linguistically, or culturally. These massive ethnic expressions represented the emergence of civil society and were far more the product of Soviet history than any primordial ethnicity or natural striving for self-determination. Whatever the intentions and predictions of self-styled Marxist internationalist officials and theorists, the actual history of most of the major Soviet peoples has been one of greater consolidation of ethnic nations, heightened national consciousness, and increased capacity to act in defense of their perceived national interests. Even the processes that had been understood by Marxists and liberals to undermine nationality – urbanization, industrialization, mobility, secular education – worked in complex ways to make nationality stronger within the pseudo-federal Soviet state. Gorbachev provided an opportunity, by pulling back state power, for the open expression of nationalist agendas, which had been shaped both by the experience of peoples in the Soviet period and by the possibility of recovering histories that had been broken off seventy (or forty) years earlier.

Beginning with Karabakh, the first year of the new nationalist movement, however, proved to be only the first round in an intensifying struggle of nationalities for greater power and autonomy. The chronic economic stagnation fed the discontents of all Soviet citizens, which were often expressed in the language of nationalism. At the same time the political demands of the nationalists and the conflicts between ethnicities accelerated the economic decline of the country.

The dramatic mobilization of Armenians and Baltic peoples in 1988 ended the long period of benign neglect of the nationality question. While Moscow might have preferred that this "problem" await its considered solution in the repeatedly delayed Central Committee plenum on the nationality question (finally held in September 1989), the contours of the issues were being shaped by people in the streets, by ad hoc committees and their intellectual leaders, and by sensitive Communist leaders, like Vaino Valjas in Estonia and Brazauskas in Lithuania, who worked *with* rather than *against* the local popular fronts. The Baltic strategy of cooperative competition between party and popular front contrasted with the harsher policy of martial law, arrests, and shootings in Transcaucasia in 1988–1989. Eventually in Transcaucasia as well, the regime was forced to accommodate itself to the growing nationalism. In neither the Caucasus nor the Baltic were state policies able to end the national movements, and as the country entered the 1990s the very survival of the Soviet Union was called into question.

The thrust of the more mobilized peoples was simultaneously toward a recovery of the past, the removal of local mafias, the end of demographic and linguistic Russification, a struggle against environmental pollution, greater local autonomy, republic-level *khozraschet* (self-financing), sovereignty, and democracy. The interests of the non-Russians could no longer be sacrificed on the altar of economic development. For Estonians this meant an end to placing plants in their republic and importing Russian workers without the agreement of the local people. For Uzbeks it could mean the end of exclusive planting of cotton, so necessary for Soviet independence from foreign cotton, but ruinous to the land, resources, and diversity of the economy in Uzbekistan. Though ethnic conflict and nationalism cannot be crudely reduced to economic causes, part of the toxic mix that produced ethnic discontent was prepared by the chronic material shortages and slow economic development of the whole country. At times Kremlin leaders appeared to hope wistfully that their policies of economic stimulation, if blessed by the fruits of prosperity, would dampen the ardor of the nationalists. In his visit to Vilnius to convince Lithuanians that their best future lay within the Soviet Union, Gorbachev spoke of the integration of the Soviet and Lithuanian economies while Lithuanian demonstrators held their national flag aloft and sang patriotic songs. While economic progress certainly might have helped, the transition to a market economy promised only greater dislocations in the near future and a greater danger that material and psychological discontents would be expressed in ethnic struggles.

The axes of conflict within the USSR were not only between Russians and non-Russians but between various non-Russian peoples who have had long religious, cultural, or territorial disputes. The

Abkhaz–Georgian hostility of 1977–1978, which revived in 1989, was a foretaste of the more tragic Azerbaijani–Armenian clashes a decade later. In Central Asia the expectations of many Western observers of a unified Muslim response to Soviet colonialism evaporated as Uzbeks attacked Meskhetian Turks and clashed with Tajiks and Kirghiz. But particularly vexing was the bleeding wound of Karabakh, the first major ethnic challenge to Gorbachev and one that resisted solution. Rather than granting the Armenian demand of incorporation of Karabakh into Arménia – a political impossibility after the killings in Sumgait – a program of reforms was set out that implicitly recognized the long record of Azerbaijani discrimination against the Karabakh Armenians. Even more importantly, Azerbaijani sovereignty over Karabakh was replaced de facto by the appointment of a commission from Moscow to oversee the implementation of reforms in the autonomous region. Expectations were raised that Karabakh might be elevated to the level of an autonomous republic, though the precise rights of autonomous regions, autonomous republics, and union republics had not yet been legally elaborated. In his interventions in the Supreme Soviet debate on Karabakh, the General Secretary made it clear that both stability and progress, the goals of perestroika, were undermined by nationalism and ethnic conflict. Only political compromise offered a solution. Repeatedly affirming that there could be no winners and losers at the expense of another ethnic group, Gorbachev pushed hard for satisfying some grievances of each of the parties. But as the authority of the local Communist parties evaporated and the nationalist fronts grew in influence, Gorbachev attempted in frustration and anger to crack down on the emergent social forces.

Following the devastating earthquake of December 7, 1988, the Soviet authorities arrested the Karabakh Committee and leading Azerbaijani militants in an attempt to restore authority to the discredited Communist parties and to gain time for the implementation of a solution from above. In January 1989 Karabakh was placed under the direct rule of Moscow. Though this compromise satisfied neither the Armenians nor the Azerbaijanis, it was thought that it permitted some "breathing space" for the passions and hostilities of the past year to settle. Compromise and calls for calm, however, failed.

By the fall of 1989 the renewed Azerbaijani Popular Front (APF) gained enormous popularity and power in the republic. On September 4, the APF called a general strike in the republic, demanding recognition and a declaration by the Supreme Soviet of Azerbaijan that the republic was sovereign. Six days later the Communist Party of Azerbaijan capitulated to the Front and signed an agreement recognizing its legitimacy. Through the fall the Front organized a rail and road blockade of Soviet Armenia and Karabakh, thus cutting off over 80 per cent of fuel and food to the Armenians. Rebuilding of the areas damaged by the earthquake came to a halt. At the September plenum of the Central Committee, which was dedicated to the nationality question, Gorbachev spoke out in no uncertain terms; "We will not depart from the path of solving all problems by means of political methods, but where the critical nature of the situation dictates it, where there is a threat to people's lives and safety, we will act decisively, using the full force of Soviet laws." The reference to Azerbaijan was clear to all. But at the same time he once again reiterated his view that the forms and borders of national entities should not be changed. His proposed alternative was the creation of a true federation in which the nationalities would have real guarantees of autonomy and local power.

Fighting continued through the fall and winter in Azerbaijan and Karabakh. At the same time there were flare-ups of nationality violence in Georgia, Moldova, and Central Asia. The Baltic republics moved decisively toward declaring their independence from the Soviet Union. For reasons that remain a mystery, the Supreme Soviet of the USSR decided to return Karabakh to the jurisdiction of Azerbaijan (November 28). Neither side had been satisfied with the administration from Moscow, and the Kremlin hoped to end the continuing blockade of Armenia by making a major concession to Azerbaijan. The Soviets showed extraordinary restraint in the face of growing militancy in Baku and Nakhichevan. Azerbaijanis tore down border guard posts and walked into Iran. Soviet power essentially no longer functioned in the republic. The local Communist Party was either impotent or actively collaborating with the nationalists.

The Armenian Supreme Soviet declared Karabakh to be part of the republic of Armenia. In all but name the two republics were at war. While Gorbachev was preoccupied with the secession of the Lithuanian Communist Party from the CPSU, violence exploded in Baku. On January 13, militants broke away from the large demonstration led by the Popular Front and began killing Armenians and burning their bodies. At least twenty-five people died the first night. Leaflets called for the expulsion of all Armenians from the city. Moscow began sending reinforcements of internal security troops by January 14. The next day a state of emergency was declared, and the army was sent in. Within the week Baku was occupied and an uneasy calm was imposed on the republic. The party chief, Vezirov, was dismissed, and the Soviet authorities arrested those nationalists considered too militant. Backed by the Soviet army, the Azerbaijan Communists, who took up the cause of Karabakh, were given a new lease of life, while the Popular Front fell into disarray.

In Armenia the struggle between the nationalists and the Communists ended in a rout of the Communists. Popular elections brought the Pan-Armenian National Movement (HHSh) to power, and a non-Communist, Levon Ter Petrossian, was elected chairman of the Supreme Soviet. Armenia was declared a sovereign state, the Republic of Armenia (Haiastan), and Ter Petrossian began the restoration of order in the republic by integrating the paramilitary forces into the ranks of the police.

As 1990 came to an end, the fissiparous nationalism within the republics threatened not only the USSR as a whole but the integrity of many of the republics. In November the ultra-nationalist Roundtable, headed by former dissident and political prisoner Zviad Gamsakhurdia, won a decisive majority in the Georgian elections. Non-Georgians in the republic faced a future of difficult negotiations and struggle. In Moldova Soviet troops were forced to intervene when the Gagauz, a Turkish people, declared themselves independent of the republic, and the Slavic peoples living near Ukraine also set up their own political authority. Three different ethnic "republics" asserted their legitimacy in Moldova, with the Soviet army trying to keep the peace.

Though predicting the future of what was the USSR has become a dangerous if popular practice for Sovietologists and journalists, any discussion of the origins and contours of the emergence of Soviet nationalism must include some analysis of the possible scenarios that exist for the near future. The first, least likely, would be a return to the pre-Gorbachevian order, a return to party oligarchy, centralization, and an imperial relationship between Moscow and its constituent nations. Though this scenario remains a utopian dream for some communists, who have imbibed the deeply conservative legacy of Stalinism, without another *coup d'état*, supported with more determination by the army and the police, a return to the recent past remains impossible. The popular mobilization, the loss of faith in the old ideology, and the lack of any program of the Right to restore the Soviet economy make a Stalinesque or Brezhnevian vision completely unrealistic.

A second possible scenario is the one increasingly envisaged in the

West and by many Soviet nationalists towards the end of 1991 – the complete breakup of the Soviet Union, full independence for the non-Russian republics, the creation of a dozen or more sovereign states. This would mean the end of empire, though not necessarily the triumph of democracy. In several of the non-Russian republics authoritarian and national chauvinistic tendencies are paramount, and the minorities that live in Georgia, Moldova, or Uzbekistan, Azerbaijan or even Lithuania, are fearful about their future in countries dominated by the majority nationality. In Azerbaijan, Tajikistan, Uzbekistan, and Turkmenia, the old Communist elites remain in control of the republics and have effectively tamed the potentially more democratic oppositions. In Georgia the policies of the popular but authoritarian president, Zviad Gamsakhurdia, have created armed confrontations, not only with the Abkhazians and Osetins, but with many of his former Georgian allies. A scenario predicting fully sovereign independent states is a real possibility, but it not only neglects to consider how sovereignty in our world has come to mean much more politically and economically limited and circumscribed state actors but it also underestimates the forces pulling the newly independent republics back toward some form of integration. Much neglected in many Western analyses has been the appreciation of the forces that bind the extremities of the former Soviet Union together into a single entity – most importantly the interdependence of the economy, but also the far-flung Soviet diaspora (25 million Russians live in the non-Russian republics; 60 million Soviet citizens live outside their home republic) and the multinationality of many of the Soviet republics (Armenia is most homogeneous at over 90% Armenian; Lithuania and Russia are also quite homogeneous at about 80%, but even they, like most republics, have significant minority populations).

A third scenario, and the one that I consider the most likely at this moment, is the partial breakup of the Soviet Union: full independence for the Baltic republics, possible unification of Moldova with a more democratic Romania, but the unity of the three Slavic republics with Central Asia and Transcaucasia on the basis of confederation. Here empire would be combined with democracy. The new, smaller confederation would be a voluntary union, based on great internal political, cultural, and economic autonomy for the republics and regions of the new "state." The republics would delegate power to coordinate economic development, military security, regulation of inter-republic relations, mediation of ethnic problems, and possibly foreign policy to a central authority. Like the evolving European Community, so the post-Soviet confederation would be a suprastate authority, coordinating and persuading, representing the collective interests of the individual republics to the outside world. How tight or loose this union might become would depend on factors too varied and difficult to predict – the perceived dangers stemming from further disunity, threats from outside, economic and security benefits from unity, the success or failure of the central bodies to promote the welfare of the republics, and the internal politics of the republics themselves.

Gorbachev remained for a long time, both practically and symbolically, the representation of unity and coordination. He was forced by events to defend a polity that he had never envisioned. Had he acted earlier, more consistently, and more courageously on the national question, he might well have saved his revolution-from-above from self-destruction. Karabakh was, as the demonstrators proclaimed on their signs, a "test for perestroika," but it was one that Gorbachev failed.

Time, unfortunately, was not on Gorbachev's side, even if history proves to be. For much too long he believed that the future shape of the Soviet Union could be dictated from the center, when that possibility had passed forever. As he lost momentum and credibility because of his hesitant coalition politics, Gorbachev's political rival, Boris Yeltsin, managed to appropriate the national issue by promising full sovereignty to the republics. It is his vision, fraught with the possibility of still further division and fragmentation as autonomous republics and unrepresented peoples assert their right to sovereignty and self-rule, that now presents both opportunities and danger.

Full democratization is the only real alternative to empire in the Soviet Union. But democracy is subversive to all forms of domination, and the reconstitution of legitimate authorities has become the fundamental problem for both the center and the republics. The consequences of democratization threaten greater instability and violence – the image of Yugoslavia stands before the eyes of the peoples of the former Soviet Union – but there is no turning back without losing the best chance in nearly a century for a freer, more democratic life.

NOTES

1 For discussions of the concept of empire, see S. Eisenstadt, *The Political Systems of Empires* (1963); his essay, "Empires," in *The New International Encyclopedia of the Social Sciences* (New York, 1968), pp. 41–49.

2 Zbigniew Brzezinski, "Post-Communist Nationalism," *Foreign Affairs*, 68: 5, Winter 1989/1990, p. 2.

3 "Nationalism and Social Class in the Russian Revolution: The Cases of Baku and Tiflis," in Ronald Grigor Suny (ed.), *Transcaucasia, Nationalism and Social Change: Essays in the History of Armenia, Azerbaijan, and Georgia* (Ann Arbor: Michigan Slavic Publications, 1983), pp. 239–258; "Tiflis, Crucible of Ethnic Politics, 1760–1905," in Michael F. Hamm (ed.), *The City in Late Imperial Russia* (Bloomington: Indiana University Press, 1986), pp. 249–281; *The Making of the Georgian Nation* (Bloomington and Stanford: Indiana University Press and Hoover Institution Press, 1988); *The Baku Commune, 1917–1918: Class and Nationality in the Russian Revolution* (Princeton University Press, 1972).

4 Suny, *The Baku Commune*, p. 14.

5 This, indeed, is the argument of much of my work on the republics of Transcaucasia. See, for example, Ronald Grigor Suny, *Armenia in the Twentieth Century* (Chicago, CA: Scholars Press, 1983); *The Making of the Georgian Nation*; "Nationalist and Ethnic Unrest in the Soviet Union," *World Policy Journal*, 6: 3, Summer 1989, pp. 503–528.

6 Moshe Lewin, *Lenin's Last Struggle* (New York: Pantheon Books, 1968).

7 James E. Mace, *Communism and the Dilemmas of National Liberation: National Communism in Soviet Ukraine, 1918–1933* (Cambridge, MA: Ukrainian Research Institute, 1983).

8 Zvi Y. Gitelman, *Jewish Nationality and Soviet Politics: The Jewish Sections of the CPSU, 1917–1930* (Princeton University Press, 1974).

9 This point has been made most effectively in the work of Sheila Fitzpatrick.

10 Aleksandr M. Nekrich, *The Punished Peoples: The Deportation and Tragic Fate of Soviet Minorities at the End of the Second World War*, trans. by George Saunders (New York: W.W. Norton, 1978).

11 In 1959, the first post-Stalin census showed that only two nationalities with their own Soviet republic, the Kazakhs and the Kirghiz, made up less than a majority of the population of their own republic, and only the Kazakhs were outnumbered by Russians:

Republic	Percentage of titular nationality	Percentage of Russians
RSFSR	83.3	83.3
Ukraine	76.8	16.9
Belorussia	81.1	8.2
Uzbekistan	62.2	13.5
Kazakhstan	30.0	42.7
Georgia	64.3	10.1
Azerbaijan	67.5	13.6
Lithuania	79.3	8.5
Moldavia	65.4	10.2
Latvia	62.0	26.6
Kirghizia	40.5	30.2
Tadzhikistan	53.1	13.3
Armenia	88.0	3.2
Turkmenistan	60.9	17.3
Estonia	74.6	20.1

(Tsentral'noe statisticheskoe upravlenie pri Sovete ministrov SSSR, *Itogi vsesoiuznoi perepisi naseleniia 1959 goda SSSR: Svodnyi tom* [Moscow: Gosstatizdat, 1962], pp. 202–208)

12 The long tenure of first secretaries in the Central Asian republics encouraged illegal activity and cronyism. In Uzbekistan, Sharaf Rashidov ruled from 1959 until his death in 1983; in Tajikistan, Jabar Rasulov ran the party from 1961 until his death in 1982; Turdakun Usubaliev was party chief in Kirghizia from 1961 to 1985; Dinmukhammed Kunaev headed the party from 1964 until his removal by Gorbachev in December 1986; and Mukhamednazar Gapurov headed the Turkmen Communist Party from 1969 to 1985. In the Soviet west the situation was not dissimilar: Petr Masherov in Belorussia (1965–1983), Ivan Bodyul in Moldavia (1961–1980), I.G. Kebin in Estonia (1950–1978), August Voss in Latvia (1966–1984), and P.P. Griškavicius in Lithuania (1974–1987).

13 Yochanan Altman, "A Reconstruction, Using Anthropological Methods, of the Second Economy of Soviet Georgia," (Ph.D. dissertation, Centre of Occupation and Community Research, Middlesex Polytechnic, 1983); Gerald Mars and Yochanan Altman, "The Cultural Bases of Soviet Georgia's Second Economy," *Soviet Studies* 35: 4, October 1983, pp. 546–560.

14 In the USSR today there is a Moslem society which is united by the bonds of history, culture, and tradition. The fact that Homo Islamicus asserts himself in Daghestan or Tashkent, in the city or the country, raises a serious problem for the Soviet regime ... Homo Islamicus is not an adversary. He does not set himself up as an enemy of the Soviet system, which he does not even criticize. But simply by his existence, by his presence in the whole area where the Moslem civilization has existed, he bears witness that the Soviet people has at least two components: the Soviets and the Soviet Moslems. (Hélène Carrère d'Encausse, *Decline of an Empire: The Soviet Socialist Republics in Revolt*, trans. by Martin Sokolinsky and Henry A. La Farge [New York: Newsweek Books, 1979], p. 264.

Michael Rywkin disputes this sharp dichotomy:

The Soviet Homo islamicus does in fact display some characteristics of his Russian counterpart unless he is among the minority who live in the most remote villages with no contacts with the Russians and practice Islam in the most traditional way, with all its rituals. For the bulk of Soviet Muslims, it is impossible to remain totally unaffected by Soviet Russian reality, and this results in multiple social identities. Thus, for example an Uzbek may view himself as Uzbek, as Turkestani, as Muslim, and as Soviet depending on circumstances and the person (or persons) with whom he deals or converses. (*Moscow's Muslim Challenge: Soviet Central Asia* [Armonk, NY: M.E. Sharpe, 1982], p. 106).

15 *Izvestiia*, August 14, 1988, p. 6; *Current Digest of the Soviet Press*, 40: 33, September 14, 1988, pp. 7–8.

16 Francis X. Clines, "Gorbachev assails Foes of his Plans," *The New York Times*, June 20, 1990, p. A6.

3 From democratization to disintegration: the impact of perestroika on the national question

GAIL W. LAPIDUS

A world ends when its metaphor has died. It perishes when
its images, though seen, no longer mean.
Archibald MacLeish

Introduction

The accession of Mikhail Gorbachev to the Soviet leadership, and the inauguration of an increasingly far-reaching program of reforms, precipitated the emergence of mass nationalism as a major political force. It unleashed an unprecedented tide of protests and demonstrations across the entire territory of the USSR in which national grievances, fueled by economic unrest, occupied a central place. It launched a process of political mobilization, and the creation of new socio-political movements, in which common nationality formed a crucial bond. It was accompanied by outbreaks of communal violence which left in their wake both loss of lives and hundreds of thousands of refugees. It precipitated violent clashes between local populations and local authorities and the use of military forces to reestablish control. And it decisively transformed the very nature of the "national question" in Soviet political life, not only bringing it to the top of the political agenda but altering the very premises of the discussion. The "national question," in the form in which it had been inherited from the past, ceased to exist. Its place was taken by a major political struggle over the nature and future of the Soviet federal system, in which sharp cleavages extending to the very top of the Soviet leadership became entwined with the broader struggle over reform.

This struggle, moreover, increasingly engaged republic elites as major political protagonists. The struggle for national rights was progressively transformed into a struggle for states' rights, as republic after republic proclaimed their sovereignty, and over time, their full independence, and fought to expand their control over political and

45

economic life within their boundaries, as well as their relations with other states. An attempted coup in August 1991 represented a last desperate effort to preserve the union in the face of mounting separatism. Its failure sealed the demise of the Soviet system and with it that of the Soviet empire, paving the way for the emergence of a series of new states on the Eurasian continent.

Ironically, none of this was either intended or anticipated by the Soviet leadership when it first inaugurated the process of political and economic reform. Even when Gorbachev's policies ignited the "national question" he and his associates continued to underestimate its explosiveness. Not until 1988, prompted by mounting inter-ethnic strife, did Gorbachev identify nationality policy as "the most fundamental vital issue of our society."[1]

Nor were reform-minded scholars or intellectuals outside the political establishment any better prepared. By contrast with the discussions of political and economic reform which long antedated Gorbachev's accession to power, the "national question" was largely absent from their agenda.[2] Only when the events of 1986–1988 shattered the complacency which enveloped intellectuals and policy-makers alike did a serious analysis and debate on the nature and future of the Soviet federation take shape, and by then events were already outpacing the leadership's ability to shape them.

The transformation of the "national question" was first and foremost a product of changes in the nature of the Soviet regime itself.[3] In attempting to revitalize the Soviet system, Gorbachev's reforms initiated what was, in effect, a major regime transformation: a transition – however limited and fragile – from post-totalitarian authoritarianism toward a liberalization[4] and incipient democratization of the Soviet system. A critical threshold was crossed when the perception of system crisis within the Soviet political elite reached a degree of urgency that resulted in a shift of power to a reformist segment of the ruling Communist Party, which moved to consolidate its position by seeking political support from social forces previously excluded from political roles.

In seeking to tap the sources of vitality, dynamism and innovation that had developed outside the framework of official institutions, Gorbachev's reforms progressively expanded the boundaries of legitimate economic, social, and political activity. The changes initiated from above created novel opportunities for the emergence and mobilization of new social actors. In particular, the official endorsement of glasnost and democratization significantly altered the relationship of state and society, legitimizing new forms of expression and activity, expanding the resources at the disposal of new groups, and altering the calculus of costs and benefits associated with political activism.[5] In effect, by curtailing the activities of the repressive apparatus of the state and thereby transforming the structure of political opportunities, the reforms were the critical catalyst in mobilizing a variety of grievances and providing them with new forms of expression.

Cognitive liberation: the impact of glasnost

During the first three years of the Gorbachev era, the progressive broadening of the scope of glasnost, which was the dominant feature of the reform process from 1985 until the spring of 1988, served as a catalyst of a revival of national consciousness that extended to virtually every region of the country. The delegitimation of Stalinism, closely linked as it was to the espousal of glasnost and of a socialist pluralism of ideas, gave official sanction to increasingly sharp critiques of Stalinist nationality policies (or indeed, to any practices that might be so labeled). It also called into question the entire gamut of assumptions, institutions, and values that had formed the core of Soviet nationality theory and policy over many decades, and nurtured the hope – and indeed the expectation – that long-standing grievances and injustices would now be rectified. Gorbachev's explicit acknowledgement, in the wake of mounting inter-ethnic tensions and conflicts, that Soviet scholarship had presented an excessively rosy view of Soviet achievements in national relations, his call for greater truthfulness in analyzing real problems, and his explicit support for filling in the "blank pages" in Soviet history, were taken as authoritative permission to reopen controversial issues of nationality policy previously closed to discussion.[6]

In the national republics as in Moscow, the extension of glasnost to the national question opened the door to an ever-widening public discussion of highly sensitive issues, a virtual outpouring of long-suppressed resentments, and growing demands for fundamental policy changes. Under the umbrella of glasnost, what had been an Aesopian dialogue among intellectual elites was increasingly transformed into publicly articulated demands by newly emerging cultural and socio-political movements devoted to national revival, which adopted names like "Awakening," "Rebirth," and "Revival" to convey their goals.

Out of an amorphous mixture of resentments and grievances that found growing expression in the local media, as well as at scholarly and cultural gatherings, the cultural and intellectual elites of the national republics began to elaborate an increasingly coherent critique of a whole gamut of Soviet nationality policies, based on an interpretation of the Soviet experience that directly challenged the prevailing official myths. In effect, the void created by the collapse of official Soviet ideology was rapidly filled by newly constructed national myths that offered a radically different interpretation of the Soviet era. This process of "cognitive liberation" was accompanied by a reframing of key issues that sought to legitimize national self-assertion by identifying it with the processes of reform and democratization initiated by the party leadership itself.

Moreover, this effort to reshape and transform collective consciousness within the national republics had affective as well as cognitive dimensions; marches, rallies, and demonstrations to mark important events in the history of the respective nation, or to protest specific government actions, made powerful use of the symbols of nationhood. Flags, hymns, holidays all served to evoke emotional commitments to the cause of national revival, and to give increasing substance to what were for many decades largely "imagined communities."[7]

In virtually all republics, among virtually all nationalities, several themes occupied a central place in this emerging discourse, although their specific form and salience would vary from one to another. A first and central theme in the struggle for national revival involved the recovery of national history. In a widely acclaimed novel entitled *A Day Lasts More than a Hundred Years*, the Kirghiz writer, Chingiz Aitmatov, drew on an ancient Central Asian folk epic to create a powerful symbol of the deliberate destruction of memory – and with it, of identity – as an instrument of rule. Aitmatov's *mankurt* became, in the Soviet context, a powerful metaphor for de-nationalization. The struggle to recapture historical truth was a struggle to restore self-knowledge, bringing historical rectification to the center of the process of national revival.

By contrast with official Soviet historiography, dissident historians of the non-Russian nations have typically presented a more ambiguous assessment of the costs and benefits of incorporation into the Russian empire or Soviet state, minimized the influence of Russian and Soviet culture on national traditions, and stressed the valuable contribution of their own cultures to the multinational one. While these themes had found some limited expression in previous decades, in the more permissive environment created by glasnost they were taken up with increasing frequency and directness not only in scholarly writings but also in the mass media. While the specific issues differed from one republic to another, certain broad themes formed a common thread.

The Stalin era repressions – the false accusations, purges, deportations, and deaths – were a first and virtually universal theme. Glasnost permitted the public exposure of mass graves whose existence had been quietly known by local populations but were for decades veiled in secrecy. It allowed discussions of the scale of repressions and deportations, as well as demands for the rehabilitation and compensation of victims. But the very essence of Stalinism was understood differently outside Moscow. Stalinism was perceived and portrayed not merely as a particularly brutal system of political repression which extended impersonally throughout the USSR, but as a form of national oppression as well, indeed as a deliberate effort to annihilate specific nations and national cultures.[8] To the "punished peoples," uprooted and deported *en masse* from their national homelands, the repressions represented the forcible destruction of national existence itself. For others, the repressions were perceived to be specifically targeted at national political and cultural elites. To Kazakh or Ukrainian nationalists, the devastating impact of agricultural collectivization was not merely an unintended consequence of misguided economic policies but arguably a deliberate attack against an entire nation.

Glasnost also opened an assault on prevailing Soviet myths concerning the process by which various nations had "joined" the Russian and Soviet empires. It rekindled controversies over boundaries and territorial claims as well as over the nature of the federal system.[9] While some of these discussions were directed at Russian imperial expansion, others involved longstanding animosities among non-Russians. The discussions extended to the history of the Russian empire as well; Central Asian historians, for example, demanded a more truthful accounting of the process of forcible conquest which had brought the region under the control of the tsarist government.[10]

The most sustained and bitter struggle over historical rectification – a struggle with unmistakable political implications – was conducted by elites and activists in the three Baltic republics to force the Soviet leadership to acknowledge publicly the secret protocol of the Molotov–Ribbentrop pact of 1939 and its role in the forcible Soviet annexation of the Baltic republics during World War II. The full text of the secret protocol was published for the first time in the Soviet Union in the Estonian language in 1988, a full year before it was published in *Pravda*. The campaign initially met with the standard official denials, as leading officials in Moscow asserted that the existence of the alleged protocol could not be proven as no original documents existed. A series of articles, conferences, and reports in the Baltic republics documenting the events of 1939 in rich detail eventually paved the way for the creation of a special commission of the newly elected Supreme Soviet to examine the question. In August 1989, in an effort to preempt the findings of the commission, as well as planned commemorations of the event in the Baltic republics, the leadership was compelled to acknowledge the signing of the secret protocol – and subsequent revisions to it. But it continued to deny that there was any connection between the protocol and the subsequent accession of the Baltic republics to the USSR, and insisted that the entire agreement had been voided by the German attack on the USSR in 1941.

The defense of national languages and cultures was another critical theme in this new discourse, as glasnost brought to the surface deep resentments against linguistic and cultural Russification. In a rising tide of speeches and articles, leading cultural figures attacked "national nihilism," lamented or deplored the erosion of their national languages and cultures, which, they asserted, were in danger of atrophy or outright extinction, and pressed for measures to restore their status and role.

Boris Oleinik, a noted Ukrainian poet and secretary of the Ukrainian Republic Writers' Union in Kiev, deplored the fact that in Ukraine and Belorussia the opportunity for parents to choose the language of instruction for their children was limited by the simple fact that in some cities "there is simply nothing to choose from – there just aren't any Belorussian or Ukrainian schools there."[11] In Kishinev, the capital of Moldova, Moldovan was reportedly among the foreign language courses taught at a local polytechnical institute.

Possibly the single most outspoken attack on linguistic Russification to appear in the Soviet press during this first phase of glasnost was an article by Mati Hint, a noted Estonian linguist. Comparing the Soviet espousal of bilingualism to tsarist and Nazi attempts to eradicate Estonian national consciousness, the article asserted:

Before the current gust of glasnost, talk started up again about the Estonians' [need for] bilingualism, naturally not with the goal of Russifying them; but for some strange reason, the apologists for bilingualism use the same arguments as the pan-Slavists and pan-Germanists: Estonian does not allow access to world culture, and without a knowledge of Russian an Estonian cannot become cultured ... The campaign, in which it is obnoxiously repeated that bilingualism must become the norm for every Estonian, creates suspicions about whether we are not dealing here with the question "To be or not to be?" Do we have the right and the opportunity to live and to do what we do and survive in the language that we have had since birth and through which we see the world? Or is it believed that even thinking about such questions is narrow-minded and nationalistic, that such questions are secondary?[12]

Indictments of Russification and its absurd, and sometimes tragic, consequences became a central theme of meetings of republic writers' organizations. At a writers' congress in Uzbekistan, a well-known Uzbek poet recalled having to help an Uzbek shepherd gain admission to the offices of the Uzbek Central Committee because the receptionist could not understand him. He reminded his listeners that if they became ill in Tashkent, or if their home were to catch fire, they would be unable to get help by telephoning in Uzbek. The editor of the Uzbek Pioneer journal underlined the problem. In answering hundreds of letters concerning a new language law, his journal had made a point of addressing the replies in Uzbek, only to have all of them returned by the post office with the injunction, in Russian, "Ukazhite adres!" ("Indicate the address!").[13]

Resentment at needing to use Russian to communicate with bureaucrats in Uzbekistan was compounded, in the view of some Central Asian writers, by the absurdity of communicating with other Turkic peoples through Russian. Alluding to the vast region which had once shared a cultural heritage, one author noted that before the revolution Turkic newspapers written in Arabic script could increasingly be understood by readers from Kazan on the Volga to Herat in Afghanistan and Izmir in Turkey. Central Asian, Moldovan, and Azeri cultural leaders pointed to the ways in which the shift to Cyrillic scripts had cut their nations off from their cultural roots and their literary classics, shaping an ever broadening agenda of language reform.

In Ukraine, where the cultural elite was sharply divided between a heavily Russified segment, largely concentrated in the eastern region of the republic, and a cultural milieu more sympathetic to the cause of national revival in the western region, the advocates of cultural revival were obliged to fight a battle on two fronts simultaneously. On the one hand, they criticized pressures for Russification emanating from Moscow. At the same time, it was essential to win over, or to discredit, unsympathetic members of the Ukrainian cultural and scholarly intelligentsia itself. At the Congress of Soviet Writers in Moscow in June 1986, Boris Oleinik directed his criticism at Ukrainians themselves, whom he held responsible for the sorry state of the national language and culture. The distortions, he affirmed, were perpetrated by "local, native, home-grown enthusiasts of our political orthodoxy who obviously inherited [their] servile psychology from those who were given allotments of their own native land for the price of speaking broken Russian. Do I have to say that this kind of nihilism categorically contradicts the nationalities policy of our party?" Oleinik went on to say: "I would ask of our Russian friends only one thing – to review quietly the mandates of those who, in the name of the Russian people, are active in the national republics to the point of forgetting who they themselves are. This, if only to convince ourselves once again of the genius of the Leninist postulate – namely, that the worst great-power chauvinists were always non-Russians (*inorodtsy*)."[14]

Ultimately, language issues were entwined with issues of status and equality. For the first time, objections to the whole conception of the "elder brother" as patronizing, if not downright insulting, began to be publicly voiced. A Siberian Evenk writer eloquently captured these sentiments when he wrote: "Thanks to all the Soviet peoples for their fraternal help ... However, we have outgrown the children's trousers and no longer need to be under guardianship. Give us the right to take charge of our destiny."[15] For many Russians, however, such sentiments smacked of an inexplicable and unwarranted ingratitude, and complaints about the growth of "Russophobia" began to fill the media. As cultural protest began to transform itself into political demands, and as newly emerging national movements called for legislation to mandate broader use of the language of the titular nationality within their republics, they confronted mounting resistance from advocates of undiminished priority for Russian.

Just as discussions of historical and cultural issues took on a distinctive meaning in the national republics, the discussion of economic reform unleashed by the process of perestroika was itself given a new twist outside Moscow. The reassessment of Soviet economic performance and policies initiated in Moscow had unleashed a wide-ranging critique of the command-administrative system, and had prompted the elaboration of economic reforms which entailed some decentralization of economic decision-making to enterprises. Scholars and public figures in a number of republics – particularly the Baltics – not only expanded the reformers' critiques of Soviet institutions and policies; they linked them to novel proposals to transfer substantial economic powers and resources to the republics.

Three themes in the discussion of economic problems had particular resonance for local elites.[16] First and foremost was the critique of departmentalism: the tendency for central economic ministries to

behave as virtual empires, pursuing their narrow departmental interests without regard to broader national needs. From the perspective of
the republics, the extreme over-centralization of the Soviet economic
system had vitiated the very meaning of federalism. Central ministries
were allowed to accumulate inordinate power and resources in their
hands, to treat the entire territory of the USSR as a single, personal
domain, and to ride roughshod over local economic, social, and ecological needs. The ministries were accused of siting industrial plants
without serious consultation with local authorities; of importing large
numbers of workers from outside the republic, upsetting delicate
demographic balances in the process and threatening to make the
titular nationality a minority in its own homeland; of making no
provision for social or cultural infrastructure for its workers, forcing
overburdened municipalities to deal with the consequences; of
ruthlessly extracting mineral and energy resources and transferring
them outside the republic without adequate recompense; and of pol-
luting rivers and poisoning the air without regard for the health and
welfare of future generations. In effect, the command-administrative
system treated territory as if it were a factory floor rather than a
nation's home.

Drawing on the argument of economic reformers in Moscow that
only a sense of mastery over the production process would assure the
effective use of resources (an argument intended to support transferring some state property into collective or private hands), scholars
and public figures in the Baltic republics asserted that enhanced
economic productivity and efficiency could be achieved only by giving
republics effective control over their own economies.

A second element of the emerging debate over center–periphery
economic relations was the controversy over "dependency" (izhdiven-
chestvo). In calling for new economic policies that would establish a
closer link between economic performance and rewards, the Gorbachev leadership had blamed excessive egalitarianism for creating an
atmosphere of dependency. Much of the criticism was specifically
targeted at the Central Asian republics, where the disparity between
productivity and living standards was alleged to be particularly great.
But by castigating both individuals and republics for failing to contribute to the national economy as much as they received, thereby
implying that some were, in effect, being subsidized at the expense of
the rest, the leadership unwittingly triggered a massive eruption of
mutual recriminations. As one Soviet commentator summed it up:
"Now everyone wants to know who is feeding and clothing whom."[17]

The entire debate was an unproductive one: the statistics tossed about were too inadequate to illuminate real resource flows, and all calculations were in any case rendered meaningless by the irrationality and arbitrariness of the Soviet price structure. But in this highly charged controversy over the relative contribution of each republic, grievances over economic and pricing policy were publicly aired for the first time, as virtually every republic claimed its contributions were undervalued, and its rewards exaggerated. Nonetheless, the entire debate brought the issue of center–periphery revenue flows into the glare of glasnost, fueling demand for republic self-financing, if not complete economic sovereignty, and forcing the whole issue of redistribution into the arena of public debate.

In virtually every republic, environmental concerns also figured prominently in the debates over economic policy. Protests directed against particular projects or practices – whether industrial plants producing dangerous pollutants, nuclear power installations, nuclear testing, or the use of dangerous pesticides – gradually expanded into broader environmentalist coalitions which joined ecological to national concerns. While no discussion of the sensitive issues of nuclear power in the aftermath of Chernobyl were initially permitted in all-Union mass media, the Ukrainian writers' journal became a forum for speeches and articles expressing concerns about the unreliability, and dangers, of nuclear power. The development of an anti-nuclear movement in Ukraine in the aftermath of the Chernobyl disaster illustrated the way in which potent new political coalitions could be forged around economic and environmental issues by linking them with national sentiments.

Political mobilization: the impact of democratization

With the inauguration, in the spring of 1988, of a new stage of the reform process, which centered on the democratization of political life and the introduction of competitive elections, the new intellectual currents nurtured by glasnost coalesced into political programs identified with embryonic new political movements. In the Soviet setting, it was predictable that these new organizations, initially unofficial and informal but over time developing into structured socio-political movements, would be overwhelmingly, although by no means exclusively, national movements. Although the emerging political range embraced a broad spectrum of causes and orientations, including Liberal-Democratic, Christian, Social-Democratic, monarchist, and

"Green" movements, common nationality and shared historical grievances were among the most powerful of all potential bonds, and the
scale of the national republics and density of ties among their intellectual elites offered a natural basis for organization.

The most innovative and politically significant of the new organizations were the popular fronts, which originated in the Baltic
republics in the spring of 1988 and within the next year had spread,
with some variations, to virtually all the republics of the Soviet Union.
The popular fronts had their roots in a proposal circulating in reformist
intellectual circles in Moscow in the spring of 1988 to create a nationwide political movement, embracing both Party and non-Party
members, which could serve as an umbrella uniting all supporters of
perestroika without directly challenging the Party's monopoly of
power.[18] The proposal foundered on the failure of the reformers to
give adequate weight to national attachments, a failure, we have
argued, shared by reformers and Party leaders alike. The creation of
mass political movements in support of perestroika would take place
not on an all-Union basis but within the framework of national
republics, and around programs in which civic orientations were
inextricably entwined with ethnic ones.

The emergence of the popular front as a prototypical new political
movement had its origins in Estonia in the spring of 1988, with the
creation of the People's Front in Support of Perestroika.[19] The idea
quickly spread to Lithuania and Latvia, facilitated by close contacts
among national activists in the three Baltic republics, and then – in a
Soviet version of the international demonstration effect – to Moldova
and the Transcaucasus.

In virtually all cases, the initiative in creating these movements came
from the cultural and scholarly intelligentsia, with members of the
republic Union of Writers repeatedly playing a central role. Historical
tradition and functional role made this group the quintessential bearer
of national culture, and even in adverse conditions it had traditionally
provided a large part of whatever dissident political and cultural
activity could be carried on. Ironically, among the unintended consequences of Soviet patterns of modernization was the vast expansion
of the scale and weight of this group.

Its leading role in the events of 1988 was further facilitated by the
release of significant numbers of former dissidents from prison or exile
– including many sentenced for national dissidence – and their
re-entry into political life. The return of Andrei Sakharov from exile to
political prominence as a consequence of Gorbachev's courtship of the

intelligentsia had its counterparts in virtually all the national republics. Indeed, an important part of the leadership of the new political movements traced its roots to the dissident activities of the 1960s and 1970s; for many, the Helsinki Committees, or the ecological protests, had served as a training ground.

Not only did the reforms provide exceptionally propitious conditions for the intelligentsia's activity, conferring upon it new status and opportunities, while curtailing the role of the KGB. Their pivotal position in the network of public communications at a time when information was emerging as a major political resource gave them direct access to a constituency of potential sympathizers as well as recruits. Their status could only be enhanced by the processes of delegitimation and democratization, which in varying degrees discredited important segments of the incumbent political establishment in virtually every republic.

The distinctive feature of the popular fronts – and the key dilemma they faced – was the tension between civic and ethnic orientations. On the one hand, they defined themselves as progressive political movements in support of perestroika. The expansion of glasnost and democratization, the defense of human rights, freedom of religion, support for pluralism, and the rule of law were all treated as essential features of a new, democratic political community. Reflecting their ecumenical approach, the fronts embraced Party as well as non-Party members, sought to attract members of all nationalities residing in their republics, and promised respect for the rights of national minorities and support for their cultural development.[20]

At the same time, the popular fronts were deeply committed to the defense of national rights and to reversing the effects of decades of Russification. The right of a nation to self-determination in its homeland was the starting point of their programs, and constituted the rationale for proposals to elevate the status of the national language vis-à-vis Russian, to restrict immigration, to establish republic citizenship and corresponding political rights, and to combat various forms of Russification.[21] The balance to be struck between civic and ethnic orientations was a central dilemma for all the popular fronts. The extent to which the interests and rights of all residents of the republic would be subordinated to those of the titular nationality would become a major source of internal conflicts.

Parliamentarism and the emergence of the federal question

The emergence of a new, if rudimentary, parliamentary system following the 1989 elections opened a third stage in the reform process. The elections not only gave enormous impetus to the process of political mobilization; they also had far-reaching consequences for the structure of power in the Soviet system, the role of the Communist Party, and the nature of center–periphery relations. Several features of the process deserve to be singled out because of their important consequences for nationality policy.

First, the very decision to initiate competitive elections accelerated the process of political organization at the local level and provided an umbrella of legality and official sanction to a variety of groups at the margin of the political spectrum. While many officials both in Moscow and in the republics sought to constrain the process, and to harass or exclude new groups, reformers within the political establishment supported a broader definition of acceptable political activity and offered tacit or open support. Moreover, because the commitment to political reform also embraced the goal of creating a state based on the rule of law (*pravovoe gosudarstvo*) which would protect individual and group rights, the overt role of the KGB in the suppression of political dissent was simultaneously circumscribed.

Secondly, the introduction of competitive elections significantly altered the position of the Communist Party in Soviet politics, relativizing its role in the political system and undermining its monopoly of political organization by subjecting it to political competition. Party officials previously accountable for their performance only to superior Party organs were now obliged to stand for election by a wider local constituency, including non-Party members. By compelling local Party officials to become responsive to local constituencies, the political reforms gave unprecedented leverage to organized local groups and accelerated the fragmentation of the Party along national lines.[22]

Not only were Party organizations of different republics at odds with each other; growing national tensions within republic Party organizations, exacerbated by struggles between conservatives and reformers at the center, were making it increasingly difficult to maintain Party unity and discipline in the face of conflicting pulls. The problem became particularly acute in the Baltic republics and Moldova, as the radicalization of the popular fronts brought increasing pressure to bear on Party organizations to back their programs or risk losing popular support. As segments of the Party leaderships formed virtual coalitions with the fronts, a number of Russians and members of other non-titular nationalities in these republics expressed growing outrage at what they considered their leadership's deviation from Party principles, and formed counter-movements to defend their interests. The most dramatic challenge to Party unity came in Lithuania, whose Communist Party – further emboldened by political developments in Eastern Europe – declared its independence from Moscow. Refusing to acquiesce in this decision, the center threw its support to the minority of Party loyalists, composed primarily of ethnic Russians and Poles, in effect sanctioning the open split of the Party into two competing organizations.

Growing fragmentation within republic Party organizations along ethnic lines was entwined with, and further exacerbated by, the growing split within the Party as a whole over Gorbachev's reforms. This conflict erupted openly at the 28th Party Congress, where disillusioned reformers threatened a massive wave of resignations from the Party if their views did not prevail, while conservatives assaulted Gorbachev for his departure from Party values.

The process of democratization was also accompanied by a progressive shift of political initiative from the Party to legislative and governmental bodies. In the republics as at the all-Union level, the newly elected parliaments were no longer content to serve as rubber stamps; they viewed themselves as genuine arenas of public debate and policy-making, and as the vehicle for the legitimate expression of republic interests. Concomitantly, the political elites of the national republics emerged as increasingly visible and influential actors in the unfolding struggles over power and policy, viewing and presenting themselves as the defenders of republic interests against the center. The growing self-assertion of the republican parliaments set the stage for a major constitutional struggle over whether republican legislation would henceforth take precedence over all-Union laws. A battle to define the nature of the federation, and the ultimate source of sovereignty, was clearly under way.

The final ingredient in this set of developments was the emergence of the Russian Republic itself as an independent and influential political actor, prepared to challenge the center's monopoly of political, economic, and cultural life. Under the leadership of Boris Yeltsin, the RSFSR not only identified itself with the program of political democratization and economic marketization from which Gorbachev was retreating in the fall and winter of 1990; it defended the republics' right to self-determination up to and including secession, and called for a fundamental transformation of the union premised on the sovereign powers of its constituent republics.

The Russian Republic's declaration of sovereignty in the summer of 1990 was a major historical turning point in all these developments. No longer could other sovereignty-minded republics be accused of nationalist narrow-mindedness and attacked with comparative impunity. The stance of the Russian Republic leadership provided an umbrella of legitimacy and protection to all the others, and created novel opportunities for coalition building among republics directed against the center.[23]

Taken together, glasnost and democratization unleashed a simultaneous cognitive and political revolution which transformed the nature of Soviet politics and, in the process, the "national question." By contributing to the erosion of the core values and institutions which had long served as the integrating forces in the Soviet multinational system, Gorbachev's reforms brought into question the entire definition of the Soviet political community and compelled a reassessment of the nature and future of the Soviet federation itself.

"New thinking" on the national question

The mounting challenge to traditional views of the "national question" – which constituted, in effect, a form of "new thinking" as well as a new discourse about nationalism and national identity – called into question many of the key premises of Soviet nationality policy as traditionally defined.[24] First and foremost, it called into question the entire myth of internationalism which had long provided the ideological underpinnings of Soviet nationality policy. The point of departure of new thinking was the explicit abandonment of the myth that the "national question" could be once and for all time "solved." For several decades, Soviet policy was based on the expectation that modernization and socialism would automatically erode national identities and loyalties and promote the creation of a new multinational community based on the equality, prosperity, harmony, and growing uniformity of its members. Such illusions were now being dispelled; as Soviet rhetoric made clear, the focus on "solving" (*reshenie*) the national question was increasingly replaced by a focus on "managing" (*upravlenie*) it.

This shift went hand in hand with the growing recognition that Soviet policy had itself contributed to exacerbating national relations. Whether the problems had their roots in Lenin's own faulty approach to the issue of nationalism, as some scholars and activists now alleged, or whether they derived from Stalinist distortions of Leninist principles, as others insisted, the whole Soviet record was now up for reassessment.[25]

In the fierce debates that now raged over nationality policy a whole series of longstanding assertions came under attack. The notion that the Soviet socialist system had destroyed all vestiges of the tsarist "prison of nations" was challenged by the argument that the USSR was an empire even more oppressive than its predecessor. The allegation that socialism had promoted both economic development and equality among nations was challenged by bitter argument over who was exploiting whom. The very notion of Russians as benevolent "elder brothers" was attacked as a patronizing effort to disguise the reality of Russification and assimilation, leaving Russians to complain bitterly of this unprecedented and unjustified wave of Russophobia.

Another important feature of the new thinking about nationality issues was the novel value now attached to national distinctiveness. The traditional view that *sliianie* – the convergence and ultimate fusion of nations and nationalities – was both a possible and a desirable goal of Soviet policy came under attack; the disappearance of national diversity, it was now argued, would constitute an irreparable human loss.[26] Gorbachev himself expressed concern for national values in affirming, in January 1989, that " ... we cannot permit even the smallest people to disappear, the language of even the smallest people to be lost; we cannot permit nihilism with regard to the culture, traditions and history of peoples, be they big or small."[27]

The new concern with re-discovering, reviving, and protecting national groups and their cultural heritage not only repudiated earlier assimilationist goals; it attached new value to the national republics as a framework for defending national values and identities. During the Brezhnev era, advocates of circumscribing the powers of the republics, if not eliminating them altogether, were on the offensive. The emergence of the republics as major political actors because of perestroika meant that this position – while retaining powerful adherents – could no longer go unchallenged. Indeed, the growing assertiveness of the republics was bolstered by novel legal arguments which insisted that sovereignty itself was vested in them and only partially ceded to the center. These new claims represented, in effect, a demand for transforming the highly centralized Soviet system into a federal or even confederal system.

The new value attached to diversity was also linked with the repudiation of a striving for uniformity. Recognizing that a country as vast and diverse as the USSR could not be treated as a monolithic whole, reformers called for the development of differentiated policies suited to the distinctive features and needs of different regions of the country. The decentralization of decision-making would in any case result in increasingly diverse patterns of economic, political, and cultural life, and different kinds of ties between center and periphery. How these variations could be accommodated within the framework of a single political, economic, and legal universe, and how republic sovereignty could be joined to the retention of important functions by the center, now emerged as a major focus of political debate.

One of the most striking and novel elements of this "new thinking" was the emergence of a specifically *Russian* national consciousness within the Russian Republic itself, focused on the demands for a full range of Russian political, economic, and cultural institutions distinct from all-Union institutions. Where traditional Russian nationalism had been closely identified with imperial aspirations, and had treated the preservation of centralized Soviet power as a primary goal, this new current aspired to the creation of a Russian nation-state as an equal partner in a reconstructed Soviet federation of sovereign republics.[28]

The major dilemma raised by "new thinking" on nations and nationalism, and a dilemma which proved exceptionally divisive for reformers, was how to address the conflicting claims for national self-determination by the union republics and by sub-republic national groups. The Inter-Regional Group, influenced by the views of Andrei Sakharov and Galina Starovoiteva, tended toward the position that only by giving equal recognition to all claims for national self-determination could the invidious hierarchical structure of national groups established by Soviet rule be overcome. Other reformers, however, feared that this approach, by weakening the rights of the union republics, played into the hands of the center. In their view, measures to enhance the rights of national minorities (such as the Law of Secession adopted by the Supreme Soviet on April 3, 1990, which permitted autonomous republics and even "compact national groups" to hold separate referendums on secession) were designed by the central authorities to thwart in practice the right to national self-determination of the titular nationality of the union republics.

Underlying the struggles between traditional and reformist assumptions about nations and national identity were two contending visions of the Soviet future. Although no simple correlation can be established, reformers, on the whole, came to view the USSR as a confederation of sovereign national republics which should enjoy substantial economic and political autonomy in shaping the destiny of their historical homelands. The center, in this view, should carry out only those limited functions of foreign and security policy, and of overall economic coordination, delegated by the republics. Conservatives, by contrast, assigned highest priority to the preservation of a powerful Soviet state based on a high degree of economic and political integration, and were fundamentally hostile to what they viewed as dangerous centrifugal forces. They viewed the entire territory of the Soviet Union as "our common home," argued – by analogy with the American model – that the individual rather than the national group was the proper subject of political rights, and insisted there should be no corner of Soviet territory in which a Soviet citizen could not feel at home. Both conservatives and reformers were themselves divided, the former over the tension between imperial and Russian national aspirations, the latter over the tension between national and human rights.[29]

Between these two scenarios, the "European" and the "American," stood a third, centrist position, advocated by Gorbachev himself and embodied in the draft of the new Union Treaty. It proposed a significant reorganization of the USSR into a federation of national states, whose subjects would include not only the fifteen union republics, but the autonomous republics as well. While a powerful central government would still shape the main lines of foreign and domestic policy, and coordinate a broad range of all-Union activities, a new formula for power-sharing would devolve significant responsibilities and resources to the republics.

Gorbachev sought to use an all-Union referendum to mobilize popular support for his approach and to discredit the advocates of more far-reaching republic sovereignty or independence, accusing them of seeking the breakup of the Soviet state.[30] In the course of the campaign leading up to the referendum, he was also obliged to come up with new rationales to legitimize its preservation. In response to earlier challenges emanating from the Baltic republics, Gorbachev had appealed to economic self-interest, emphasizing the extensive economic interdependence of the various regions of the USSR and the high costs of disrupting these ties. As individual republics sought to expand their ties to foreign partners in the quest for capital, markets, and expertise, Gorbachev insisted that the expansion of these economic ties depended on political stability and predictability, the preservation of a single national market, and the undisputed authority

of a strong central government. He also warned repeatedly of the
dangers of ethnic conflict and "Lebanonization" should central power
be seriously weakened. Most telling, perhaps, was his increasing
reliance on traditional forms of historical legitimation, focusing not
merely on the achievements of Soviet power but on the entire course
of Russian history as an argument for preserving the present state:

> Our "yes" will preserve the integrity of a state that is 1,000 years old and has
> been created by the labor, intellect, and innumerable sacrifices of many gener-
> ations. Of a state where the destiny of peoples, millions of human destinies,
> our destinies are inextricably interwoven.

> Our "yes" means respect for the power (*derzhava*) that has repeatedly proven
> its ability to uphold the independence and security of the peoples who are
> united within that power.[31]

But the results of the referendum did little to strengthen Gorbachev's
hand. Six republics refused to conduct it altogether, holding separate
polls to demonstrate strong popular support for independence, while
the results in the remaining nine revealed that the strongest support
for preservation of the union came from the more rural and less
developed regions of the country, particularly the Central Asian
republics. In some of the urban regions of Russia and Ukraine close to
half the voters voted "no."

By the spring of 1991, therefore, the political situation had reached a
stalemate. The attempted crack-down in Vilnius in January 1991 made
it clear that Gorbachev could not impose his own vision of a Soviet
federation, and preserve the territorial integrity of the union, without
the use of substantial coercion, which would erode his international
and domestic support further, and aggravate the economic crisis,
without resolving the fundamental issues. The republics, however,
while capable of obstructing the implementation of central decrees,
still lacked the economic and political infrastructure essential to
autonomous existence. As Yeltsin described the situation of the RSFSR:

> We have no power. Here we just discuss and adopt resolutions, and we do not
> know whether they will be carried out, because they have all the real power.
> They have the administrative, state, and Party apparatus, the army, the KGB,
> and other structures. We have none of this.[32]

From union to commonwealth: the August coup and its aftermath

In an effort to reduce his dependence on the conservatives, and to find
a political compromise which would break the perceived impasse

between the center and the republics, Gorbachev met on April 23, 1991 with the leaders of the nine union republics, including Boris Yeltsin, and negotiated what became known as the "9 + 1" agreement – in effect, a new center–left coalition premised on a confederal arrangement. Over the next few months, a new draft of a Union Treaty was hammered out which involved substantial concessions to the demands of the union republics for greater political, economic, and military powers, and for control over key central functions, above all taxation and budgeting.

The mounting alarm of the conservatives over what they perceived as the imminent destruction of the Soviet state came to focus on the planned signing of the new Union Treaty on August 20, 1991.[33] In an effort to avert what they portrayed as the impending betrayal of the fatherland, a coalition embracing elements of the military, secret police, central Communist Party apparatus and military-industrial complex attempted to establish emergency rule. The defeat of this attempted coup by a democratic opposition rallied by Yeltsin discredited and undermined the remaining institutions of central Soviet power, and accelerated the shift of power from Gorbachev to Yeltsin and from the center to the republics. Above all, it signaled the end of the union.

The Ukrainian referendum of December 1, 1991 constituted the final act of the unfolding drama. Recognition of the independence of the three Baltic states in the aftermath of the coup was largely a foregone conclusion. There remained the expectation, however, that some elements of economic, political, and military union among the remaining republics could be preserved, and that with the Ukrainian presidential campaign behind him, the Communist-turned-nationalist Leonid Kravchuk would be prepared to reach a compromise. Gorbachev plunged into the effort to preserve the union with renewed vigor, seeking to enlist Western governments on its behalf. These expectations were dimmed by the evident disarray among the republics, and dashed by the proclamation of independence by Ukraine. In a desperate effort to avert the prospect of a dangerous breach between Russia and Ukraine, Yeltsin seized the opportunity to reach a dramatic agreement with Ukraine and Belarus on the creation of a new Commonwealth of Independent States to replace the former Soviet Union, and then to open its membership to the five Central Asian republics and others who might wish to join. Proclaiming the end of the Soviet Union, Yeltsin requested diplomatic recognition of Russia as its legal successor.

These rapid and momentous developments have created only the broad framework for a radically new set of political arrangements. A protracted period of negotiation and coalition-building will be necessary before a number of outstanding problems are resolved.

A first set of issues involves the relationship of the newly proclaimed independent states and the commonwealth, and the delineation of their respective jurisdictions. The new arrangement envisions only limited coordination of the policies of the member states, primarily in the military and economic spheres. Yet even here, the provisions for a unified command of nuclear forces or for the preservation of a "common economic space" will require detailed delineation of respective jurisdictions. There remains considerable potential for frictions over the scope and structure of military forces, or over the way in which coordinated economic policies and open borders can be combined with the desired degree of economic autonomy of states with vastly divergent economic resources, priorities, and needs.

These issues are in turn entwined with uncertainties concerning the very durability of the new commonwealth arrangements. Whether the commonwealth will turn out to be a transitional arrangement to cushion the road to full independence, or whether it will define for itself a valued and enduring role in balancing the diverse interests of its members remains an open question, but managing the intricacies of these relationships will demand at a minimum exceptionally skillful leadership.

The potential sources of conflict among members of the commonwealth are further magnified by unresolved territorial and border disputes, and by the presence of substantial minority populations, especially Russians, outside what will now become Russia's state borders. Should Russians in the Baltic states, or in Ukraine or Kazakhstan, for example, come to feel their status or security seriously threatened, their discontent could have a destabilizing impact on the entire region. Whether as a result of large-scale migrations, or appeals for support and assistance, or the emergence of powerful right-wing Russian nationalist movements, their political fates are inextricably entwined with the fate of the fragile democratic institutions in Russia itself.

Finally, the territorial integrity of the Russian state is itself being challenged. How the Russian government will handle growing demands for autonomy – and even for independence – voiced by nations and even regions of the RSFSR remains an open question.

Moreover, separatist strivings among some of the nationalities of the Caucasus are likely to be given additional impetus by the emergence of independent Muslim states along Russia's southern borders. Whether the Russian government will repeat the mistakes of the former union in resorting to coercion, as was almost the case in Chechen-Ingushetia, or whether it will find more promising approaches to these issues, will have far-reaching consequences for the stability of the entire region.

Whatever the fate of the newly emerging arrangements, the entire map of Eurasia has been irrevocably altered by the events of the past few years. Having emerged as major political actors because of the Gorbachev reforms, the former republics of the Soviet Union are now transforming themselves into increasingly sovereign states with a growing capacity, as well as desire, to manage their own political, economic, social, and military affairs autonomously. They have been creating an increasingly dense network of horizontal ties no longer channeled through, or mediated by, Moscow. And they have become more and more active in seeking out foreign economic partners and cultivating foreign support for their aspirations, as well as seeking inclusion in a variety of international organizations and fora. Forcibly cut off for many decades from regions outside Soviet borders with which they shared deep historical, cultural, and economic ties, they are now engaged in restoring those links, the Baltic states with Scandinavia and northern Europe, Ukraine with Eastern and Central Europe, the Central Asian states with Turkey and the Middle East, and the Russian Far East with the countries of the Asian Pacific region. Over time, the former republics of the Soviet Union are likely to become increasingly different from one another, politically, economically, and culturally, and to draw closer to different communities outside their borders.

The entire process we have been witnessing has no real analogs in Western historical experience. Not only is the simultaneity of the transition from authoritarianism and from a command to a market economy historically unprecedented; it has been joined to an equally unprecedented combination of state breakdown, decolonization, nation-building, and the formation of a new supra-national community. As these newly emerging states renegotiate their relationships to each other, to their own populations, to the new commonwealth, and to the larger international community they will undoubtedly create unprecedented challenges and dilemmas, as well as opportunities, for all concerned.

NOTES

1 Speech to the CPSU Central Committee, February 18, 1988; *Pravda*, February 19, 1989.
2 While the constraints on empirical social research made it difficult to challenge the prevailing mythology concerning national relations, Soviet intellectuals themselves tended to be critical of nationalism as an atavistic phenomenon, and assumed that modernization would erode national identities and loyalties, and replace them with new supra-national attachments. They expected that a shared commitment to economic and political change would unite reformers across the Soviet Union.
3 The deterioration of Soviet economic performance was undoubtedly a critical factor in aggravating inter-ethnic tensions and conflicts, in provoking communal violence, and in encouraging separatism, but widespread Soviet beliefs to the contrary, it was not the primary cause of the problems.
4 Post-totalitarian authoritarian systems share a set of distinctive ideological, economic, and socio-political features which distinguish them from traditional forms of authoritarianism, in which capitalist economies provide the basis for a significant degree of institutionalized social and political pluralism.
5 For a more extended treatment, see Gail W. Lapidus, "State and Society: Toward the Emergence of Civil Society in the USSR," in S. Bialer, ed., *Politics, Society and Nationality Inside Gorbachev's Russia* (Westview, 1989).
6 For example, Gorbachev's speech to the January 1987 Central Committee plenum included an acknowledgement that the problems brought to the surface by the demonstrations of December 1986 in Alma Ata were hardly confined to Kazakhstan, that the Party had committed real errors in nationality policy, and that the taboos which prevented serious discussion of these issues only exacerbated them. Blaming scholars for presenting excessively rosy assessments of Soviet reality, he called upon social scientists to conduct serious analyses of nationality problems (*Pravda*, January 28, 1987). It fell to a well-known author of precisely such rosy assessments to spell out the critical implications of this speech for nationality theory. In a major article in *Pravda*, Eduard Bagramov of the Institute of Marxism-Leninism presented a critique of key features of traditional approaches (August 14, 1987).
7 The evocative phrase is that of Benedict Anderson from *Imagined Communities: Reflections on the Origin and Spread of Nationalism* (London, Verso, 1983).
8 The powerful anti-Stalinist film *Repentance*, for example, typifies the tendency to subsume Stalinism into a broader portrait of tyranny in general just as the organization of *Memorial* was intended to embrace all victims of repression. Cultural elites in non-Russian republics, however, tended to view Stalinism through the prism of their particular national experiences.
9 It encouraged Armenian elites to reassert their claim to Nagorno-Karabakh on the grounds that Stalin had arbitrarily violated arguments which assigned the territory to Armenia; it prompted Moldovan activists to reclaim territory transferred to the Ukrainian SSR during World War II; in

short, it revived innumerable territorial conflicts throughout Soviet territory that had lain dormant in more repressive times.

10 See, for example, the discussions at the meeting of the Kirghiz Writers' Union on June 23, 1988; and of the Uzbek Writers' Union on June 24, 1988; *Radio Liberty* 309/88 July 12, 1988.

11 Speech to Congress of People's Deputies, *Izvestiia*, June 2, 1989.

12 *Edasi*, May 29, 1987, cited in *Radio Liberty/Baltic Area Report*, July 17, 1987.

13 *Radio Liberty Report*, 1: 38, September 22, 1989, p. 17.

14 *Literaturna Ukraina*, July 3, 1986, as translated in *Radio Liberty Report*, 270, July 8, 1986.

15 Alitet Nemtushkin, "Stoit li mnozhit' oshibki?" *Sotsialisticheskaia industriia*, June 28, 1988, as cited by Marjorie Balzer, "Intelligentsia in Transition: Sources of Yakut Identity," Paper prepared for US/USSR Conference on Ethnicity, 1989.

16 For a more extensive discussion see Lapidus, "Gorbachev and the 'National Question': Restructuring the Soviet Federation," *Soviet Economy*, July–September, 5:3, 1989.

17 *Moscow News*, April 3, 1988, p. 12.

18 Boris Kurashvili, Tatyana Zaslavskaya, and Fyodor Burlatsky were among the advocates of such a movement; *Moscow News* and *Sovetskaia molodezh*, March and April 1988; *The New York Times*, May 24, 1988.

19 The very adoption of this title and organizational form reflected both the new opportunities introduced by perestroika and a sensitivity to Soviet norms. As Marju Lauristan, one of its founders and subsequent leaders, explained, the term "Narodnyi front," with its populist and unifying connotations, was deliberately chosen over the potentially divisive "Natsional'nyi front" to emphasize the civic orientation of the movement (*Sovetskaia estoniia*, March 13, 1988, p. 3). Moreover, the term has a favorable historical resonance in the Soviet vocabulary, evoking a historically legitimate and progressive form of political organization which, in Western Europe in the 1930s and after World War II in Eastern Europe, embraced both Communists and non-Communists on behalf of a common cause.

20 The extent of the efforts made, and the degree of which they in fact succeeded in these efforts, varied considerably. For example, 14 per cent of the early members of the Latvian movement were ethnic non-Latvians, by contrast with the membership of Birlik, its Uzbek counterpart, which was almost exclusively Uzbek.

21 The Estonian program served as a prototype of subsequent programs, although each embraced provisions specific to local circumstances; for the complete text and supporting documents, see *Narodnyi Front Estonii, Khartiia programma* (Tallinn, 1988: *Narodnyi Kongress, Sbornik materialov kongressa Narodnogo Fronta Estonii*, October 1–2, 1988).

22 The dilemma of maintaining central control over local Party officials while encouraging them to be responsive to local constituencies was exemplified during the dispute over Nagorno-Karabakh: in June 1988 virtually the entire leadership of the Armenian republic supported the transfer of

Nagorno-Karabakh to Armenia, while the Azerbaijan leadership voted to retain the territory.

23 This stance in turn inhibited the ability of the central government to use military or economic leverage against recalcitrant republics. For example, an attempted crackdown in Lithuania in January 1991 was thwarted not only by Lithuanian resistance but by Yeltsin's open defiance of the attempt and his call to Russian soldiers not to use arms against peaceful civilians.

24 "New thinking" about national relations was already emerging in the Brezhnev era, as ethnographers and sociologists conducting empirical research on ethnic processes began to challenge traditional assumptions and to frame new approaches. But the obligatory tone of self-congratulation which permeated scholarly writings, and the continuing ideological constraints surrounding the entire conception of the "nation" reduced the utility of these studies in preparing either the political leadership or the public for the problems ahead. For a more extensive treatment, see the author's "New Thinking and the National Question," in Archie Brown, ed., *New Thinking in Soviet Politics* (Macmillan, London, 1992).

25 For examples of a burgeoning literature see Khallik, *Natsional'nye otnosheniia v SSSR i problemi perestroiki*, Tallinn: Dom politprosveshcheniia universiteta Marksizma-Leninizma TsKKP Estonii, 1988; Nenarokov, "Za svobodnyi soiuz svobodnykh narodov," *Istoriia i politika KPSS*, 3, 1989, pp. 3–64; Zotov, "Natsional'nyi vopros: deformatsii proshlogo," *Kommunist*, 3, 1989, pp. 79–89.

26 See, for example, the argument by a distinguished Soviet ethnographer, Sergei Arutyunov, that "any disappearance of an ethnos is a tragic phenomenon ... The concept of ethnic pluralism should have its Communist variant ..." ("Natsional'nye protsessy v SSSR," *Istoriia SSR*, 6, 1987, p. 94). The most eloquent statement of this newly legitimate view by a leading political figure came in an address to a Central Committee plenum by Vaino Valjas, First Secretary of the Estonian Communist Party, who argued that the nation is the basic form of human existence, and that national culture is the foundation of universal human values (*Pravda*, September 21, 1989).

27 *Pravda*, January 8, 1989.

28 The new discourse was predicated on the distinction (lost in the English language) between the terms "russkii" and "rossiiskii," the former referring to Russian ethnic identity and the second to inhabitants of the territory of the Russian Republic.

29 Some reformist leaders, most notably Yeltsin and Afanasyev, supported the right of national self-determination even to the point of secession, while others feared it would jeopardize perestroika itself. Reform-minded economists also opposed the fragmentation of a national market, and many believed that national tensions were largely the consequence of economic deterioration, and would be alleviated by successful economic reform.

30 *Izvestiia*, March 1, 1991, p. 2.

31 Televised speech of March 15, 1991 as reported in *FBIS*, March 18, 1991.

32 Moscow Radio, October 16, 1990; as quoted in Elizabeth Teague, "The Soviet 'Disunion': Anomie and Suicide," *Report on the USSR*, 1: 47, 1990, p. 2.
33 The alarm of the conservatives was spelled out most dramatically in the "Address to the People," in effect an appeal for support for a coup, signed by twelve military, political, and cultural figures published in *Sovetskaia Rossia*, July 23, 1991, p. 1.

4 The evolution of separatism in Soviet society under Gorbachev

VICTOR ZASLAVSKY

The nationality crisis in the Soviet Union has been the most acute manifestation of the general crisis of Soviet-type societies. Whereas the deepening economic crisis has undermined the superpower status of the Soviet Union, the nationality crisis was the main threat to the survival of the Soviet empire, which has finally entered into a period of disintegration after more than seven decades. To use a term no longer in vogue, the Soviet Union has provided us with yet another example of the dialectic of history, when the same social arrangements and policies that had served as the pillars of internal stability suddenly became counterproductive, leading to instability and profound tension.

The Soviet federal policy, based on the Stalinist definition of a nation that includes a national territory as the essential attribute, established an inseparable link between an ethnic group, its territory, and its political administration. The Soviet state successfully manipulated nationality relations by forging an administrative hierarchy of different levels of statehood which were assigned to various nationalities. A quota system was also organized which promoted the preferential treatment of indigenous nationalities within their delimited territories, regulated competition for university admissions, and restricted access to managerial and administrative jobs. Ethnic identity was transformed into an institutional reality by the mandatory registration of ethnic affiliation in internal passports. A rigid bureaucratic procedure for passing officially registered ethnic affiliations from one generation of Soviet citizens to the next was in place for more than half a century. Ethnic cohesion was promoted and reinforced by the state-mandated imposition of an officially recognized and immutable nationality on every citizen and by the creation of ethnoterritorial administrations and indigenous ethnic ruling elites.

These policies promoted a peculiar process of nation-building. On the one hand, the state imposed formal ethnic cohesion, created practically impenetrable barriers between different ethnic groups, and established an administrative link between individuals and their nationality groups. Thus there emerged in the various republics such preconditions for independent existence as political elites and educated middle classes, administratively defined political subunits inhabited by the indigenous populations, and continuous traditions of cultural production in their own literary languages. On the other hand, the Soviet state developed effective mechanisms for controlling the composition and activities of local administrations and for preventing any ethnic community from acting as a unified entity in defense of its ethnic interests.

With the advent of perestroika and the collapse of centralized control, nationality emerged as the most potent base of social mobilization. In the words of the Soviet philosopher Grigorii Pomerants: "Nationality, the only officially recognized distinction between Soviet citizens, has become a leading principle of political organization ... Nationalities have turned into political parties."[1] Accordingly, the degree of ethnic assertiveness has grown enormously, with nationalist and separatist movements emerging in most of the Soviet republics. Granted, as Paul Goble argues, ethnic activism cannot be measured by a single standard, such as demands for independence, because this leads "to a significant underestimation of the degree of national activism by groups with different problems, prospects, and agendas."[2] Nonetheless, in Soviet circumstances demands for independence have become the decisive characteristic of national relations, as even partial satisfaction of such demands will determine both the future of what was the Soviet Union as a socio-political entity and the prospects for other forms of ethnic activism.

As one of its unintended consequences, Gorbachev's perestroika laid bare and deepened the two major faults running through the structure of the Soviet empire-state. The first fault separates the three Baltic republics and Slavic republics, while the second divides the southern, predominantly Muslim, republics from the rest of the country. These two faults have engendered quite different types of nationalism and ethnic activism, both in terms of nationalist objectives and in terms of the degree of social mobilization and the types of conflict generated. An aborted August 1991 coup attempt served as a powerful catalyst in the disintegration of the USSR. It accelerated the achievement of full political independence by the Baltic republics and a further crystallization of separatist movements in some other parts of the former Soviet Union.

The Baltic republics: separatist anti-imperialism

The situation in the Baltic republics has always been characterized by separatism within the auspices of an anti-imperialist movement. The 1940 annexation of the Baltic states was followed by mass terror, the imposition of an alien socio-economic system, and deliberate state policies aimed at undermining the ethnic survival of the indigenous populations. This could only have led to the permanent politicization of ethnic identity.

The central role that educated classes and indigenous intelligentsia play in promoting ethnic mobilization and organizing secessionist movements is well known. The structural position of the educated classes which are the principal bearers of a "shared, literate, educationally transmitted culture" makes them especially receptive to the appeals of nationalism in industrial societies.[3] As Miroslav Hroch put it: "Both the old and the new middle classes become the main champions of 'nationalism,' both in state-nations and in small nations that experienced the nation-building process."[4] By protecting the educational and occupational interests of the indigenous elites and middle classes, Soviet nationality policies have been unusually successful in integrating the groups most receptive to nationalist ideas into the political regime or, at least, in neutralizing their separatist aspirations.

In the Baltic republics, however, the policy of segmenting ethnic groups by class and territory largely failed. Among the reasons for this failure one can cite the Baltic republics' small size and relatively developed infrastructure, factors that undermined territorial stratification. More importantly, the threat to ethnic survival has been so pressing and acute, especially in Estonia and Latvia, that regaining independence has become an existential demand by the entire population of the small Baltic nations. Finally, the incredible cohesion of the Baltics was cemented by strong cultural traditions and reinforced by a separatist movement that held promise for all strata of the population.

The maintenance of ethnic identity in the Baltic republics has been facilitated by the continuous development of national cultures fostered by the Soviet policy of promoting the hegemony of titular nationalities in all spheres of cultural production within their territories. The Baltic republics succeeded in achieving institutional completeness,[5] since each developed a parallel set of institutions for indigenous and Russian speakers with little communication across the language divide. Before perestroika, cultural events such as song and theater festivals, along with extensive publishing in the local language were the only tolerated means of cultural mobilization in the Baltics. In recent years, however, the Baltic ethnic mobilization quickly evolved beyond the cultural arena to encompass a rapid succession of stages, moving from an ecological movement to a nationalist activism which sought greater autonomy within the Soviet federation, and culminating in a full-fledged separatist movement. The true novelty of Baltic separatism consists of its final goal, which not only envisions secession from the Soviet Union and political independence, but also incorporation into another supranational community, be it the European Common Market, the European Free Trade Area, or even the proposed Baltic Commonwealth. Finally, the Baltic republics enjoy considerable international support for their separatist project. Historically, it was substantial external support which had allowed former parts of the Russian empire, like Finland, Poland, Estonia, Latvia, and Lithuania, to attain independence and build genuine sovereign states.[6] The assistance of the international community has become a crucial element for the successful regaining of Baltic independence.

1991 will enter history as the year when the 1989 East European "velvet revolution" engulfed the Soviet Union as well. Nowhere has this revolutionary process been more successful than in the Baltic republics.

The year began with a well-planned crackdown on the recalcitrant Baltic republics, whose timing deliberately coincided with the beginning of the Gulf War. It was, in essence, the first attempt at a military coup against democratically elected governments in the non-Russian republics. Yielding to hardliners' pressure, Gorbachev issued a strong-worded appeal to Lithuania's legislature urging it to revoke the republic's declaration of independence of March 1990. Immediately anonymous, self-appointed bodies, the so-called "national salvation committees," sprang up, first in Lithuania and then in Latvia. Soviet troops stationed in the Baltic republics backed these salvation committees and occupied local radio and television centers, while Russian migrant workers employed by the military-industrial complex and Lithuanian atomic power station went on a political strike demanding the introduction of presidential rule. But the crackdown backfired. It created an unprecedented political mobilization within the Baltic republics. Hundreds of thousands of people rose up to defend their legitimate governments. Moreover, the Baltic crackdown prompted a new consolidation of democratic forces throughout the Soviet Union. It triggered huge demonstrations in major Russian cities and mass rallies in some non-Russian republics. It accelerated a mass defection of prominent economists, intellectuals, and politicians from the Gorbachev camp. Most importantly, Western response to the Baltic repression was prompt and determined, suspending trade credits and blocking emergency food aid and technical assistance packages. The central government had to retreat and relax its pressure on the secessionist republics.

Identifying the social forces behind the Baltic crackdown in the winter of 1990–1991, Gavriil Popov, the radical mayor of Moscow, argued that its real instigators had been the Baltic republics' party apparatuses trying to regain power, with the help of the CPSU apparatus, the KGB, the army, and the military-industrial complex.[7] In this sense, it was a dress rehearsal for the August 1991 coup. The failure of the Baltic repression forced Gorbachev to reconsider his policies of using all possible means to impose a top-heavy Union Treaty on the republics and to preserve the Soviet Union's territorial integrity. In turn, Gorbachev's change of camps and his readiness to support Yeltsin's liberal version of the new Union Treaty, which would have resulted in a definite shift of power from the center to the republics, triggered another attempt by the same forces to seize power and to prevent Soviet disintegration. The August 1991 coup failed for roughly the same reasons as its Baltic predecessor. The international recognition of Baltic independence endorsed by the democratic government of the Russian republic and ratified by the then already largely ceremonial Soviet president was one of the most dramatic consequences of the coup's failure. The new Baltic states are now working on marketizing their economies and accelerating their reintegration into the world market by joining existing supranational European and international organizations.

Central Asia: amorphous ethnic activism

In contrast to the Baltic republics, the type of ethnic activism predominant in the Central Asian republics is distinguished by the virtually total absence of separatist claims. Local intellectuals are experiencing tremendous difficulties in formulating either a program of action common to Central Asia as a whole or specific programs for single republics. Ethnic conflicts in the region have a pronounced horizontal character, and ethnic mobilization remains largely spontaneous, leading to violent inter-ethnic clashes and bloody pogroms directed by indigenous populations against a variety of identifiable minorities within each republic. This is an archaic, heterophobic form of ethnic activism which has not yet reached the stage of an organized nationalist movement. The local intelligentsia has not been promulgating separatist ideals or accumulating the resources necessary for the pursuit of independence. To understand the reasons for this state of affairs one must examine the origins of the local educated classes, not to mention the organization of cultural production and distribution in Soviet society in general and its Central Asian republics in particular.

Traditional Soviet nationality policies have always pursued the goal of the structural isomorphism of all union republics, regardless of their different histories, cultures, and levels of industrial development. This meant that the production and distribution of culture was organized through such standard organizations as republican ministries of education and culture, academies of sciences, creative unions of writers, painters, architects, state publishing houses, theaters, and film studios.[8] Simultaneously, the central state apparatus implemented a policy to treat titular nationalities preferentially, thus firmly protecting the interests of the local educated classes and political elites. The emergence of numerous new middle classes in the Central Asian republics has been state-engineered and state-supported, and can only be partially attributed to the process of modernization, with its basic elements of urbanization, industrialization, the spread of mass education, and the appearance of the mass media. Indeed, to a very considerable extent, this emergence was determined by the functioning of the Soviet redistributive state and its specific nationality policies, aimed at maintaining internal stability within the multiethnic empire. The dependence on the state by the Central Asian intellectuals is clearly demonstrated by the inflated size of the group, by the over-representation of titular nationalities, and by the excessive proportion of humanistic and artistic intelligentsia in the composition of the group.

The Soviet policy to modernize and "Russify" Central Asia ultimately imposed a uniform superstructure on what nevertheless remained a relatively unchanged Islamic culture and way of life, with a general population whose habitual behavior remained that of a traditional peasant society.[9] As Edward Allworth has noted, the basic values and beliefs that pervade this society and create its attitudes have not been altered by decades of Russian rule.[10] The continuous demographic explosion may serve as the best confirmation of this. Characteristically, local intellectuals hold the central government responsible for the destruction of the environment and mismanagement of the economy. But afraid of antagonizing the Muslim population at large, they never call for extremely unpopular measures like fertility-control programs to contain the demographic growth. The proposals by some Russian demographers to make the center's assistance to these republics conditional on the introduction of family-planning programs[11] have evoked angry responses on the part of Central Asian intellectuals, who termed them racist and genocidal.

A possible transition to a market economy and the imminent secession of the Baltic republics immensely frightened many members of the Central Asian political elites and the state-dependent middle classes. Political leaders, like Uzbek President Islam Karimov, continuously demanded a return to "the Leninist principle of equalization of the levels of development."[12] The only support for Gorbachev's Union Treaty project, which was based on the principle of a strong central government, came from the leaderships of the six republics with Muslim titular nationalities.[13] As a result, a somewhat paradoxical situation emerged. The decentralization and devolution of the central state compelled local political and cultural elites to act independently in the pursuit of their own ethnic interests. But what could Central Asian elites propose in the face of a continuing demographic explosion, a spreading ecological decay, and a deepening economic crisis? The battle for promoting indigenous cadres to managerial and administrative ranks had already been won during the Brezhnev years. Another battle for raising the languages of the titular nationalities to the positions of state languages had also been won – more recently. One of the major effects of decentralization, as Wlodzimierz Brus emphasizes, is that "local interests are now able to manifest themselves not only in pressing the center for favorable allocations, but also in the promotion of development plans backed by their own resources."[14] The paradox of the Central Asian situation lies in the fact that, having few resources of their own to utilize for their own purposes, these republics ended up becoming ardent supporters of a strong center. Their local educated classes were so dependent on the central state that they simply could not participate in the organization of a separatist movement. The only feasible strategy to pursue in the short term consisted of forming a political bloc to pressure Moscow for increased investment, appealing to the historic responsibility of Russians for the current state of affairs. In view of the incessant ethnic strife in various Central Asian republics, any attempts by intellectuals to reinforce the cultural, religious, and linguistic unity of the peoples of the region and to revive the idea of an independent Turkestan looked more akin to wishful thinking than to a realistic goal.

The reaction of Central Asian leaderships to the attempted coup in

August 1991 highlighted both their political dependency vis-à-vis the center and their overwhelming economic interest in maintaining a close political and economic union with the Slavic republics, especially Russia. While the majority of members of the party nomenklatura in all Central Asian republics supported the coup, the attitudes of the democratically elected presidents of Kazakhstan and Kirghizia, who had been trying to limit or dismantle the nomenklatura rule over the respective republics, was predictably negative. As a result, after the failure of the coup, these leaders strengthened their ties with the Russian government and put their republics in the forefront of the struggle for the preservation of economic and political union between the republics. These policies could count on considerable support from the Russian populations within Kazakhstan and Kirghizia. Having established good relations with their Russian constituencies and supported Yeltsin during the coup, Kazakh and Kirghiz leaders justifiably expected more than mere moral obligations from the Russian government to maintain an economic and political union. In contrast to Kazakhstan and Kirghizia, some sort of communist counterrevolution occurred in Azerbaijan, Uzbekistan, and Tajikstan after the coup failure. In these republics the old party nomenklatura, using its control over local legislatures and the proven system of single-candidate elections, managed to preserve the one-party system and communist control. This development led to a strong antagonism between democratic forces in the center and the communist governments of these southern republics. The latter found themselves in an increasingly difficult position. On the one hand, communist leaders could rely on the support of the Russian government. On the other hand, their strong dependence on the redistributive central state and especially on Russian subsidies and markets did not permit their resorting to nationalist and especially separatist policies. Consequently, these communist governments remained fragile. The Tajik government rapidly collapsed under the pressure, while Uzbekistan's and Azerbaijan's leaders had to follow the Russian Republic in abolishing their communist parties, thus falling back on clans and kinship ties as a basis of political power.

The inability of the Central Asian intelligentsia to generate a mass nationalist movement does not mean that no such movement will emerge in the future. If a Soviet transition to a market economy is to be at least moderately successful, the Soviet redistributive state will have to be totally dismantled. The educated classes of Central Asia will soon come to realize that the investment necessary to prevent grave social dislocations will never materialize. Moreover, massive unemployment will spread among the local educated classes, whose occupational interests will no longer be protected. In fact, republican governments have already begun to reduce bureaucratic personnel. In addition, a major clash between the Russian Republic and Central Asia over ecological issues, especially the distribution of water resources, is approaching. In the future, the marginalized and frustrated Central Asian intellectuals will have little difficulty in mobilizing the population at large around ecological issues and Islamic fundamentalism. Very much will also depend on the policies of regional leaders in countries like Iran, Turkey, or Saudi Arabia and their willingness to render assistance and strengthen their respective influence in the Central Asian republics.

Russian nationalism: two contending ideologies

The cultural and political struggle in the Russian Republic and the evolution of Russian nationalism should be of particular interest for at least two reasons. First, the disintegration of the Soviet Union as a nuclear state and as a military superpower will have a profound effect upon the conduct of international affairs, and it will have political and social ramifications over the entire globe. At the same time, the direction and logic of specifically Russian nationalism will determine the eventual fate of the Russian army and nuclear forces, which have always been the principal institutions of the Soviet state. Second, the Russian Republic represents a paradigmatic case which can illustrate the major alternatives available for the transformation of Soviet-type societies.

In the late 1980s and early 1990s, the entire social atmosphere of the Soviet Union changed dramatically. As the Soviet writer Daniil Granin remarked even before the failed coup: "Socialism, once a utopian dream, has been transformed into an anti-human concept."[15] Another influential literary critic summed up the situation as follows: "Everything is colored by the impression of a shattering collapse suffered by the recently powerful Soviet civilization."[16] Many Soviet intellectuals have still been settling accounts with Marx and Lenin, and Sovietologists have also been tallying the blows suffered by the Communist Party and Communist ideology in general. Yet the real social struggle is not taking place between Communism and anti-Communism. Rather, as Adam Michnik perceptively observed, the Soviet Union provides "an especially vivid illustration of the two types of anti-Communism now locked in combat against each other."[17]

As in other Soviet republics, the nationalist idea has quickly gained the upper hand in the mass social consciousness of Russians. In the present circumstances, the Russian popular mind is rapidly becoming disabused of traditional Russian imperialist tendencies and is turning to nationalism and separatism as a result. Unlike the other republics, however, nationalism in the RSFSR is split into two contrasting ideologies that envision radically different prospects for the Russian nation. Here an analogy with the Polish situation is appropriate: "The most important conflict in Polish culture today is being fought between those who see the future of Poland as part of Europe and those characterized by the Polish sociologist Jerzy Szacki as 'natiocentric,'" writes Michnik.[18] Analogously, in Russia the combatants are those who insist on the distinctiveness of Russian development and the specific mission of the Russian people, who view "the convergence of life-styles, world view, and culture [with the West] as a shameful sell-out," and those who emphasize the unifying features of the world civilization and prefer to see Russians "as normal people living in a normal country."[19] This is nothing more than the traditional Russian conflict between Westernizers and Slavophiles, a conflict that is being replayed with intensity and intransigence unmatched in its previous incarnations. While these developments have unfolded in a remarkably brief period, one can trace their roots to events which occurred long before the rise of Gorbachev.

An early clash between the liberal-democratic, Europe-oriented anti-Communism and its xenophobic, authoritarian, anti-Western counterpart occurred in the Soviet Union in the late 1960s in the form of the ideological struggle between Russian intellectuals connected with Tvardovskii's *Novyi mir* and those grouped around the journals *Molodaia gvardiia* and *Nash sovremennik*. The history of this episode in Soviet cultural life is well known. At the time, the *Molodaia gvardiia* group took up the banner of Russian patriotism and of a "Russian party" and began to promote an extremely contradictory complex of ideas, attitudes, and stereotypes – combining their genuine anguish for the destruction of Russian culture and the peasantry, the Russian Orthodox Church, and Russian traditions with a defense of a Stalinism which was seen as the legitimate continuation of Russian imperial traditions. The notion of a Jewish or Zionist conspiracy against the Russian people accordingly helped to expiate Stalinism and shift the responsibility for the destruction of the Russian peasantry and culture from the Bolshevik regime to a small and unpopular ethnic minority. These "unenlightened nationalists," as Anatolii Strelianyi labeled them, could never decide between "a Russian revival or the preservation of the empire."[20] Instead they wanted both, and created not a Russian nationalist ideology but rather a more traditional blend of Russian nationalism and imperialism.

A number of intellectual, psychological, and pragmatic reasons can be cited to explain the emergence of that peculiar ideological combination. First, the *Molodaia gvardiia* adherents were raised in the tenets of Soviet ideology, cut off from Western philosophical traditions and the social thought of Russian emigration. As a result, they were completely in the thrall of the idea of a Manichean division of the world into "good" and "evil" and entirely susceptible to the notion of a global conspiracy, whether directed against socialism or against the Russian people. Second, they exhibited the early manifestations of a psychological mechanism that has been described by Michnik,[21] prevalent in all countries where Communists had seized power: a tendency to "hold aliens and foreigners – Russians, Germans, Jews, cosmopolites, Freemasons – accountable for bringing Communism" to the respective countries. Finally, this imperialist-nationalist ideology corresponded to the social position and perceived grievances of its creators – the members of the Russian humanitarian, artistic, and scientific intelligentsia. The occupational interests of this group were best served by defining "Russianness" solely by blood ancestry and also demanding the creation of specifically Russian organizations, such as a Russian Communist Party or a Russian Academy of Sciences. This was a reaction to the massive presence of so-called "Russified" Jews in scientific and cultural occupations, the only occupational niches open to the Jewish minority after their exclusion from the Party apparatus, state administration, the trade unions, and the military. Not surprisingly the emergence of the idea of a "Russian party" coincided with the first signs of an overproduction of specialists and a sharp intensification of job competition in Soviet "closed cities," where the Jews comprised a sizable percentage of the population.[22]

This early confrontation between the liberal-democratic and nationalist-imperialist ideologies of the Russian intelligentsia had two distinguishing characteristics. It was, on the whole, a marginal phenomenon confined to relatively small groups of intellectuals and of little import to the mass popular consciousness, as confirmed by ethno-sociological studies which found that only a fraction of the population, mainly the humanitarian intelligentsia, was aware of the ideological struggle between *Novyi mir* and *Molodaia gvardiia*.[23] Furthermore, at that time the Soviet Party leadership had a monopoly on political and ideological power, and was consequently capable of carefully monitoring the cultural life of Soviet society and keeping the conflict in check. As a result, the *Novyi mir* editorial board was replaced, while their opponents were mildly reprimanded and tacitly encouraged. This difference in treatment resulted from a tacit acceptance by the Party apparatus that Russian imperialism and chauvinism were the pillars of the Soviet state.[24]

In the new circumstances of perestroika, the liberal-democratic and nationalist-imperialist movements underwent rapid evolution and modification. They acquired new characteristics and proposed new programs; they split into warring factions and entered into hitherto unthinkable alliances, and they played for mass audiences and acquired social support in various strata and groups of Soviet society. In particular, with the advent of glasnost these contrasting ideological movements acquired a mass audience and therefore gained more room to maneuver. Initially, an original imperial nationalism had enjoyed a temporary advantage over the repression-weakened liberal-democratic anti-Communism by virtue of its arrival on the scene as a cohesive force with its own press and mass organizations such as *Pamyat*. The manifestos of this movement, such as Igor Shafarevich's *Russophobia*, have been published in huge print runs. The notion of an internal conspiracy against Russian culture, in the form of Judeo-Masonry, enjoyed a renaissance. Russian culture was being categorized by ethnic origin, with the Union of Writers splitting into unions of "Russian" and "Russian-language" authors. There was an upsurge of anti-Semitism which provoked a mass Jewish emigration, now resembling a virtual exodus. The formation of a Russian Communist Party finally occurred, with its ideology and program based on a broad amalgamation of Communist and Russian nationalist ideologies. Finally, various ideologists of Russian nationalism entered the highest echelons of Soviet administration.

Yet as this old Russian imperial nationalism attempts to enter the arena of open political struggle and formulate a program of action, the inherent contradictions of this ideology will prove to be its downfall. The period when an undifferentiated Russian nationalist ideology could hold together the "empire-savers," predominantly loyal to the Soviet state, and the "nation-builders," loyal to the Soviet nation,[25] has come to an end. Recent years have witnessed a deepening polarization of the nationalist ideologists and activists into imperialist and nationalist-separatist camps. Imperialist nationalism has been losing ground, and many ideologues of the imperialist persuasion have promptly changed their allegiance. The turn from imperialist nationalism to separatism has been promoted by changes in Russian mass consciousness on the one hand and by the growing influence of liberal nationalists and the dissemination of nationalist ideas among the Russian liberal-democratic intelligentsia on the other.

The national identity of the majority of the Russian populace has been historically based on an imperial idea. Vladimir Balakhonov said it best: " ... among Russians the imperial instinct is tremendously strong, and we cannot as yet imagine any form of existence other than our current empire, stretching from Brest to Vladivostok."[26] Balakhonov also concluded that since the majority of Russians were "many centuries removed from the experience of national discrimination," their national identity was "state-based rather than ethnic" and hence receptive to the role of enslaving other nations into the empire. As a consequence, the Russians could comprehend either the oppression of non-Russian ethnic groups in the Soviet Union or the oppression of the Russian people by the imperial state.[27] Indeed, numerous ethnosociological studies over the years invariably found that whereas the non-Russian national groups identified themselves with their republic, the overwhelming majority of the Russians identified itself with the Soviet Union, rather than Russia proper. As Yuri Arutiunian concluded, the Soviet regime had basically succeeded in making the concepts of Russia and the Soviet Union congruent in the minds of Russians.[28]

Yet by the late 1980s, the situation had changed so much that more perceptive observers began to doubt that "imperialist" Russians favored the maintenance of their multinational state. Some even predicted that "possibly the Russians might opt for seceding from the Soviet Union and creating their own national state."[29] Indeed, a drift towards isolationism and a separate Russian consciousness that began with the advent of perestroika intensified in recent times. For the first time in history, the Russian popular response to the growing assertiveness of non-Russians did not favor imperialism and chauvinism but rather the emergence of a genuine Russian nationalism that aspired toward the creation of a national Russian state.

At the same time, the Russian nationalist revival that followed the collapse of socialism assumed a peculiarly reactive character. Deluded by years of Soviet propaganda which trumpeted the enormous hardship suffered by the Russian people for the sake of the development in the backward periphery, the Russians were genuinely indignant and angry at the explosion of anti-Russian sentiments in the "ungrateful" republics. Furthermore, they were faced not with the mythical Russophobia of Shafarevich, orchestrated by Jews bent on world domination or the equally improbable Freemasons, but with palpable and increasing pressures directed at Russian minorities in the union republics (or even the Russian majority in Kazakhstan).

This pressure is now beginning to be felt on the territory of the Russian Republic because of four circumstances. First, the sharp fall in living standards has intensified ethnic conflicts over economic policy choices at the republican level and job competition at the individual level. Second, there has been a rapid growth in the importance of market relations throughout the country, more as a consequence of the deepening economic crisis than of a planned conversion to the market economy. Yet markets dealing in produce and other foodstuffs traditionally have been dominated by representatives of the southern republics. The importance of these markets in the life of all Soviet citizens, including Russians, is continually increasing; the markets appear as the main cause of inflationary price increases and consequently provide a convenient ethnic scapegoat. Third, the appearance of a large number of Russian refugees from the restive republics has made a tremendous impression on the mass consciousness of Russians. By now not only the demographers, but the populace at large has begun to realize the consequences of the Muslim demographic explosion. An important factor in this realization is military service in which the Muslim presence is large and increasing, while inter-ethnic clashes are growing in frequency and violence. Finally, ecological problems are taking on an increasingly ethnic character. For instance, in the near future one can expect new confrontations between the Russian and the Central Asian republics over the redirection of Siberian rivers towards Central Asia, a colossal project that has already been shelved once – by the Gorbachev leadership – but is now returning to the agenda.

The resolute struggle of the Baltic republics for independence produced a particularly striking impression on the Russian popular mind. The Russians came to realize that the secession of these most productive and industrially developed republics would leave them eye to eye with the rapidly growing Muslim population of Central Asia. The enormous investments required to contain unemployment and to implement large-scale irrigation projects in Central Asia could only come from the coffers of the Slavic republics, chiefly from Russia. Moreover, in the Russian popular mind the southern republics were ever more closely linked with images of corruption, organized crime, and above all inter-ethnic violence. Each day the cost exacted from the Russian population to maintain the empire was becoming more difficult to bear. As General Dmitry Volkogonov, a military aide to Yeltsin, wrote: "Russians have paid the price for their false position as 'elder brother' and for their imperial policy: they have lost their own rights and face animosity from people who see Russians as promoting the interests of the empire by the use of the bayonet."[30]

Characteristically, the harbingers of newly isolationist sentiments in Russian cities were mass protest rallies against the mobilization of Russian youths for military peace-keeping duty in Azerbaijan. These protests became so widespread that the defense ministry edict mandating the call-up of reservists was quickly countermanded. Even more characteristically, during the elections in both 1989 and 1990 candidates connected with imperial nationalism received few votes, despite support by organizations like *Pamyat* or "The United Workers' Front of Russia."

All of these developments accelerated the schism between the groups oriented towards the imperial idea and those espousing separatism and an inward-looking Russian nationalism. The ideologists directly connected with nationalist journals like *Nash Sovremennik*, *Literaturnaia Rossiia*, and *Molodaia gvardiia* had to embark on a change of course. The virulent anti-Semitic and anti-Freemason propaganda was toned down as it became clearly absurd and counterproductive to their mobilizational drive. The authors of these journals began to cast about for a more credible front of Russophobia and a more suitable scapegoat for the Russian predicament. And so, from 1989 onwards, anti-Muslim sentiments have burgeoned in Russian nationalist publications.

At the same time, the disintegration of the Soviet economy reinforced the popular perception of the high costs of maintaining the empire. The result was a "mass conversion" to the separatist creed. Thus, at the first session of the Congress of People's Deputies, the writer Valentin Rasputin jokingly proposed the secession of Russia from the Soviet Union and reaped a raucous round of laughter from deputies who appreciated his clever sally. A scant several months later the slogans of Russian separatism began to carry the day. In a total about-face, the bard of Soviet imperialism, Alexander Prokhanov, fresh from extolling the might of the Soviet forces and victories in Afghanistan, proclaimed that "The future of Russia is Russia!" and exhorted the Russians "to cast off the biting, ungrateful neighbors, to elude their growling pack and stand by ourselves."[31]

The rapturous reception of Solzhenitsyn's pamphlet "How to Build the Russian Future" among the Russian populace, and particularly among the educated classes, was largely due to his decisive support of Slavic separatism.[32] Isolationism and separatism were emerging as the one platform unifying all the major strands of Russian nationalism. Nothing illustrates this point better than the ongoing evolution of the Russian liberal-democratic intelligentsia.

In Soviet conditions, the Russian liberal-democratic intelligentsia had always concentrated its efforts on combating Stalinism and totalitarianism. The question of the specific national interests of the Russian people was generally neglected. This tendency had ample historical precedent. By the turn of the century, Nikolai Berdyaev noted that the reactionary tsarist rule had deformed the national identity of the adherents of the liberation movement, producing a revulsion against the very idea of a "nation." As a result, the democratic movement had acquired a cosmopolitan rather than nationalist character. In an article characteristically titled "Why is the Russian Democratic Movement 'Ashamed' of the National Idea?", Marina Salie, a noted democratic activist from Leningrad, explains the persistence of this attitude to this day:

All acts of vandalism perpetrated by Soviet power against minorities – from the annexation of the Baltic states, Western Ukraine, Belorussia, and Bessarabia, to the Stalinist deportations of minorities, to the occupation of Hungary and Czechoslovakia and the invasion of Afghanistan, to the discrimination against Jews and the bloody repression of the Tbilisi demonstrations by Russian troops under the command of General Rodionov – all of these acts can only provoke in the Russian intelligentsia a shudder of powerlessness before the genocidal policies, a complete alienation from the idea of liberating their own nation, and a fear of appearing nationalistic in the eyes of the democratic community within and outside the USSR.[33]

Still, in recent years the Russian intelligentsia has begun to sustain a growing awareness that the national idea need no longer be repudiated, and that Russian national interests should be addressed with the greatest urgency. Several factors contributed to this evolution. First, as Fedor Burlatsky admitted, "the national idea has become well-nigh dominant in the social consciousness of the country,"[34] and the liberal-democratic intelligentsia could not avoid its influence. Nor could the intelligentsia fail to comprehend that the battle against Stalinism and the successful introduction of democratic reforms required the mobilization of the Russian population at large. Second, the Russian intelligentsia always contained a group, albeit few in number, of liberal

Russian nationalists who perceived the evolution of Russia through the prism of an enlightened Russian self-interest, abhorred chauvinism, defined membership in the Russian nation by culture rather than blood, and viewed Russian culture as an admission ticket to world culture. The moral authority of people such as Dmitry Likhachev or Sergei Averintsev has risen markedly, while the promulgation of the ideas of liberal nationalism has been facilitated by a close cooperation with Western-style liberals.[35] Another factor responsible for the evolution of liberal nationalism has been the growing realization that even a gradual transition to a market economy is incompatible with the Soviet empire: the republics simply cannot enter the market simultaneously, given that "the political, historical, and psychological preconditions for the transition to a market economy differ widely among [them]."[36] Finally, Russian reformers in quest of profound economic and political changes could not help but turn to Russian nationalist-patriotic sentiments as a means to gaining and holding political power. While Gorbachev nominated nationalists such as Valentin Rasputin and Veniamin Yarin to the Presidential Council, Boris Yeltsin was equally adept in turning Russian isolationism and separatism to his advantage in the struggle for power. Instead of the top-heavy new Union Treaty which was backed by Gorbachev, Yeltsin's program stipulated the right of the republics to secede from the union and proposed bilateral agreements between the republics. This was a large step forward towards turning the Russian Republic into a fully sovereign republic and the Soviet Union as a whole into a voluntary confederation of self-governing republics.

It would appear that in contrast to the past, when the only grounds for consensus between Russian nationalists and the liberal-democratic intelligentsia was an appreciation of the terrible harm visited on the Russians and the Russian culture by the Soviet state, today these two groups can unite under the banner of Russian separatism and isolationism. A closer examination, however, reveals Russian separatism to be at least as contradictory as the preceding ideology of imperial nationalism. The old clash between Westernizers and Slavophiles, between patriots and cosmopolitans, has reemerged during the "agony of Soviet civilization"[37] as a conflict between two diametrically opposed visions of Russian separatism. On one side we have a separatist program based on Russian national interest, calling on the Russian people to cast off the backward, non-European, non-Christian components of the Soviet Union and to return to the home of European culture, of which classical Russian culture was an integral part. This program envisions the opening of Russia to the influences of developed industrial countries, a transition to a market economy and integration into the world market system. On the opposite side, isolationism is understood not only as separation from all non-Slavic or even non-Russian republics, but even more crucially as a repudiation of the West and a search for a specifically Russian way of life and Russian spiritual values. The Soviet literary critic Sergei Chuprinin aptly described this ideology as "Russian fundamentalism," quite akin to the Khomeini-style Islamic variety. The fundamentalist program consists of "the voluntary secession from a surrounding 'blasphemous, decadent, and gluttonous'" humanity, retreat to national self-isolation, and "the closing of the borders and the imposition of homogeneity, both social and national, on the Russian population."[38] The conflict between Russian fundamentalism and liberal nationalism is rapidly becoming a major ideological confrontation within Russian culture and society.

In conclusion, the general malaise of the Soviet system has generated a profound crisis in Russian national consciousness. This crisis has engendered political combat on two fronts. First, there has been an unceasing struggle between traditional imperial nationalism and a new movement towards isolationism and separatism. In August 1991 the imperialist hardliners set on preserving the Soviet Union as an indivisible entity suffered a crushing defeat. Although the imperialist strain appears defeated, its legacy is by no means irrelevant. The Russian imperial tradition may in the future continue to play an important role within the Soviet confederation and the Russian Republic itself. In the latter, as Anatolii Strelianyi points out, "the proportion of 'imperialists' can fall nearly to nothing and then suddenly jump to nearly a hundred percent, while an active ten percent is sufficient to get the job done."[39] Nonetheless, for the foreseeable future the major battle surely will be between Russian fundamentalism and liberal nationalism.

For its part, the imperialist tradition is entering into curious alliances with the two types of separatism. This is evident in the recent publications of such otherwise dissimilar authors as Alexander Solzhenitsyn and Alexander Tsipko. The two are brought together by the remnants of an imperial consciousness that Solzhenitsyn advocates – possibly without being aware of it – by calling for the expulsion of eleven republics from the union while, at the same time, keeping Ukraine, Belorussia, and Kazakhstan in a future Russian state, which as a result would comprise over 80 percent of present Soviet territory. In case separatist sentiments will also prevail in these republics, Solzhenitsyn proposes to redraw the present borders separating Russia from Ukraine and Kazakhstan in such a way that the territories populated by Russians within these republics would be included in the future Russian state. Attempts to exploit Solzhenitsyn's enormous moral authority in defense of the fundamentalist vision are to be expected. It has already been argued that the expulsion of the non-Slavic republics should be complemented by an isolation from "pernicious" and "corrupt" Western influences, since only in this way can Russia pursue her specific development and fulfill her special mission in the evolution of humanity. In addition, some conservative Russian nationalist organizations have already called for annexation of the Russian-populated parts of Ukraine, Moldova, Kazakhstan, and Kirghizia.[40] As for Tsipko, he opines that since the construction of the empire has been a major Russian national achievement, Russians continue to be responsible for its maintenance.[41] Tsipko's unresolved contradiction is typical of those liberal nationalists who could not fully overcome the imperial legacy. He combines the idea of the Russian responsibility for the empire with the clear understanding that the empire's future can only be based on violence and coercion. Yet he also rejects violence and, most importantly, repudiates the notion of a "unique Russian way of historical development." Like all liberal-democratic thinkers, he advocates the transition to a market economy and Western-style political pluralism.

The process of designing, justifying, and testing a program of liberal Russian nationalism has been long and protracted. The creation of a Russian national state has been encountering enormous resistance both within and outside the Russian Republic. This resistance has been shaped by the secular history of Russian imperialist expansion. On the one hand, even the most liberal approach to the secession of the union republics could not solve the problem of those republics which were unwilling to secede and whose dependence on Russia would only increase as a result of their continuing demographic growth and the progressive exhaustion of favorably located natural resources, especially water. On the other hand, the Russian Republic included several dozen nationalities and ethnoterritorial units and represented a microcosm of the Soviet Union. The same ethnic mobilization which characterized the situation in the union republics is now spreading among such lower-rank ethnoterritorial formations as autonomous republics or oblasts. Thus, during 1990, the overwhelming majority of autonomous republics have unilaterally raised their status to that of

union republic. They adopted declarations of sovereignty and proclaimed the exclusive right to the territory's natural resources. In
addition, most of them introduced their own citizenship and granted
equal rights to both the Russian language and to the language of the
titular nationality.[42]

In most cases these actions were initiated by local political elites
eager to expand their sphere of control and strengthen their bargain-
ing position vis-à-vis the center. Moreover, the titular nationalities at
large have a stake in these transformations, since the state's long-
standing nationality policy has taught them that an ethnic unit's rank
in its system of Soviet ethnic stratification determines its share of state
investment and strengthens the preferential treatment accorded to the
titular nationality.

The position of the center vis-à-vis the problem of the changing
status of regional units and the collapse of the old system of ethnoterritorial stratification has undergone a number of radical changes. Initially, Gorbachev's administration pronounced the first declarations of
sovereignty by the autonomous republics illegal and invalid. Later,
however, it began tolerating and even tacitly encouraging them. First,
the center had a vested interest in having as many ethnic subjects of
the new Union Treaty as possible, since this strengthened its position
vis-à-vis any single republic. Not surprisingly, union republics such as
Kazakhstan and Uzbekistan strongly opposed the idea of making the
former autonomous republics signatories of the Union Treaty. Second,
the center had tried to use ethnic mobilization in sub-republican ethnic
units to weaken the position of those republican governments which
demanded too much control over their economies or which fought for
full political independence. Thus, the position of the leaders of Russia
and Georgia could be effectively undermined by an alliance between
Moscow and sub-republican units located on the territory of the
Russian and Georgian republics. The failure of the coup put an end to
attempts by the center to encourage the autonomous formations
within the Russian Republic to declare their full sovereignty.
Moreover, while the authority of the Russian government headed by
Yeltsin grew immensely, many leaders of the autonomous republics
were heavily compromised by their support of the attempted coup
and rapidly dismissed.

The difficulties and pitfalls facing a liberal program of Russian
nationalism are evident. It seems, however, that the liberal-democratic
reformers from the "Democratic Russia" alliance and the Russian
republican government coalescing around Boris Yeltsin understand

the potential of the Russian national idea for mobilizing the population around their new leaders so as to introduce painful reforms. They distance themselves from more extreme proposals aimed at expelling underdeveloped republics from the union. They strongly support Yeltsin's policies of promoting Russian sovereignty, while offering a larger degree of self-rule to the autonomous republics located on the territory of the Russian federated republic. Their reform strategy combines a resolute pursuit of marketization, especially the reintroduction of private property in land, with a rapid conversion of the military into a civilian industry. These are necessary preconditions for a Soviet entrance into the world market and for future cooperation with the West which, in turn, would help initiate a new stage of "catch-up" modernization.

The reformists in the Yeltsin administration envision the future Soviet Union as a Soviet Commonwealth, understood as a loose confederation of republics pursuing marketization at their own pace. In contrast to Gorbachev, who insisted on a new Union Treaty to be imposed on the secessionist republics from above, they propose a Union Treaty evolving from below on the basis of voluntary agreements signed by the republics themselves. They also propose more realistic formulas for the new Union Treaty. It has been suggested, for example, to divide it into separate economic and political treaties. The economic treaty would create a Soviet-style common market which all republics would join out of sheer self-interest. The political treaty would be signed only by those republics which perceive it as beneficial to themselves and which agree on the new union's internal structure and on the prerogatives of its central government.

An April 1991 meeting between the leaders of the nine republics that participated in the 1991 referendum on the preservation of the Soviet Union and Gorbachev apparently resulted in a new approach to the division of power between the center and the republics.[43] Gorbachev's recognition of the right to self-determination and the promise to rely on economic leverage instead of force to maintain the territorial integrity of the country was an important change of position. This change only came about as the result of the intense pressure put on the all-Union government by the Russian leadership. This political compromise between the center and the republics, however, can hardly last for long. Given the continuous pressure on the part of the secessionist republics and the economic and demographic disparities between the three Slavic and six Muslim republics, a Slavic–Muslim federation may be maintained only by a strong redistributive central state. Russian liberal nationalism can hardly agree to the continuation of such a state and the stability of the new union will soon be put into jeopardy.

As to the multi-ethnic character of the Russian Republic itself, Yeltsin and the liberal-democratic nationalists have already begun consistently replacing the term "Russkii" (which refers to people of Russian nationality) with the term "Rossiiskii," which in modern Russian refers to all peoples residing in the territory of the Russian Republic. Taking into account the fact that the autonomous republics and oblasts have always been ethnically heterogeneous, that their degree of Russification is very strong, and that their geopolitical location is hardly conducive to the pursuit of political independence (indigenous populations recognize this fact), Russian liberal nationalists hope that large-scale marketization in tandem with the recognition of cultural rights of all peoples populating the republic will eventually dampen the acuteness of ethnic conflicts within Rossiia. Under the new conditions, a peaceful consensual change of ethnoterritorial borders or even a complete defederalization might become integral elements of a new nationality policy.[44] In sum, a program of enlightened Russian nationalism is predicated on continued close cooperation with the West combined with consistent attempts to gain the popular acceptance of marketization reforms. Liberal Russian nationalism presents itself as a non-partisan patriotic force defending the overriding interests of both the Russian nation and the peoples of Rossiia as a whole.

After the aborted coup, the Yeltsin government sought to convince the non-Russian republics to sign an inter-republican agreement which would preserve the "common economic space" by retaining common currency and central monetary institutions and by guaranteeing free trade among the sovereign republics. Grigory Yavlinsky, the nation's new chief economist, suggested that such a reconstitution of the Soviet Union would be a necessary precondition for starting an all-Union privatization program and obtaining large-scale financial aid from the Western countries. Many Western leaders also considered an agreement between the republics and the central government necessary before the West could seriously become engaged in the reform process. It was obvious that Russia, because of the immense size and large population, would again be playing a predominant role in this new union. The Russian Minister of Foreign Affairs suggested that "a democratic Russia will become a national center of gravity for the other sovereign republics."[45] But the evolution of separatism in such republics as Ukraine already convinced some observers that the idea of reconstituting the Soviet Union on new democratic foundations was no more than "the inertia of imperial thinking," as Tsipko put it.[46] The conditions and interests of the different republics were so divergent or contradictory that any central government would have been forced to continue the old policies of the redistributive central state – the very policies that needed to be dismantled if the transition to a market economy remained the major strategic goal of Soviet reforms. Some Soviet experts were beginning to realize that the creation of a new Soviet federation was impossible without the previous disintegration of the old one. As Oleg Bogomolov, economic advisor to Yeltsin, pointed out, the country had lost faith in the central authorities and even if a reform program based on preserving the Soviet federation would have been accepted by the republics, it was "very unlikely that it will be implemented."[47] Thus, in search for an ethnic structure which might become a foundation for the reformist project, liberal Russian nationalist had increasingly come to realize that the interests of the Russian population would best be served by synchronizing a gradual disintegration of the Soviet empire with the implementation of market reforms in the Russian Republic.[48] In December 1991 the leaders of Russia, the Ukraine and Belorussia, the three founding members of the Soviet Union, have pronounced the end of the USSR as a subject of international law and a geopolitical reality. They pledged to found instead a loose association or commonwealth of independent states open to the remaining republics. This has been an important step towards the realization of the program of Russian liberal-democratic nationalism. Having created this commonwealth, Russia has averted the threat that the most conservative republics would determine the tempo and the parameters of reforms. As a result, the resistance to radical economic reforms will weaken, providing better opportunities for Russian integration into the global market. Meanwhile Russia may claim to be the legal successor of the Soviet Union and retain the status of a great power despite the Soviet collapse.

The fundamentalist program occasionally appeared so obsolete, unrealistic, and almost ridiculous that many observers failed to consider it seriously. Russian isolationism, which was based on putative Russian uniqueness, could not offer any reasonable way out of the economic crisis and would have appeared to be doomed on these grounds alone. Yet it would have been unwise to underestimate the mobilizational potential of this fundamentalist project for four reasons.

First, fundamentalist isolationism furnished a program capable of uniting both monarchists and Stalinists, those who found Russian uniqueness in Orthodox religion and imperial tradition, and those who found such uniqueness in Marxism-Leninism and the socialist world order. Second, it might have rallied the broad strata of the population that would inevitably suffer in the course of marketization and the ensuing social dislocations. Fundamentalism might have proved particularly appealing to marginalized groups, including the unemployed and the Russian refugees from the peripheral republics. Third, while there appeared to be no rational alternative to the reintroduction of a market economy and reintegration in the world market, one should not underestimate the potential appeal of irrational policies. A party with a fundamentalist platform need not come to power solely through a military coup; it can also win elections in a perfectly democratic manner on the wave of spontaneous populist mobilization. Finally, although the Russian fundamentalists clearly had no practical program of economic reform and were unlikely to develop one in the future, this did not mean that they had no plan of political action. After all, if raising the Russian standard of living in absolute terms was not possible, the fundamentalists might have sought to raise it relatively by supporting the arms race or some sort of Third World dictatorship, thus depressing the stability and the standard of living of the capitalist West.

One of the leading theoreticians of Russian nationalism, Eduard Volodin, consoled himself and his readers that given "all the natural resources and industrial potential, the nuclear weaponry and the well-equipped, technologically advanced army" Russia would always remain within the ranks of the great powers.[49] In this regard, the Soviet political scientist Evgenii Ambartsumov published in *Moscow News* a parody of the reaction of the pre-Gorbachev Soviet press towards Iraq's invasion of Kuwait: "The Soviet people unanimously celebrate the victory of socialist revolution over the crumbling Kuwaiti monarchy and express their class solidarity with socialist Iraq which rendered selfless fraternal assistance to the Kuwaiti masses."[50]

What seemed to be a clever parody has proven to be much closer to reality than its author probably ever imagined. Before the beginning of the Gulf War Russian right-wing nationalist organizations like the Fatherland society or the United Workers' Front organized marches and rallies in support of Saddam Hussein and the Union of Russian Writers approved pro-Hussein resolutions by an overwhelming majority.[51] During the war Russian fundamentalists intensified their attacks on Soviet foreign policy for supporting the West against Iraq. Both Russian imperialists and fundamentalists united their efforts in accusing the Soviet leadership of betraying future Russian interests. Newspapers like *Sovetskaia Rossiia*, *Literaturnaia Rossiia*, and *Krasnaia zvezda* kept publishing articles by Russian right-wing nationalists and top-ranking military leaders which condemned the coalition troops for the aggression launched against the Iraqi people and expressed strong anti-Western sentiments. Members of the right-wing "Soyuz" bloc in the Supreme Soviet even attempted to send a delegation to Iraq to express their solidarity with Saddam Hussein. The possibility of an anti-Western alliance between Russian fundamentalism and some Third World dictatorships should not be ruled out.

There is no doubt that had the 1991 coup succeeded this would have become a major thrust of Soviet foreign policy. The triumphant appearance of Russian nationalism in the cultural and political arena was undoubtedly one of the final blows to the Soviet regime and a harbinger of the Soviet empire's disintegration. But the victory of the fundamentalist variety of Russian nationalism not only portends new suffering for the Russian people, but can exert a strong destabilizing influence on a global scale.

NOTES

1 Grigorii Pomerants, "Po tu storonu zdravogo smysla," *Iskusstvo kino*, 10, 1988, p. 26.
2 Paul Goble, "Moscow's Nationality Problems in 1989," *Radio Liberty Report on the USSR*, 2: 2, 1990, p. 13.
3 Ernest Gellner, "The Dramatis Personae of History," *East European Politics and Societies*, 4: 1, 1990, pp. 131–132; Ernest Gellner, *Nations and Nationalism*, Ithaca, NY: Cornell University Press, 1983.
4 Miroslav Hroch, "How Much Does Nation Formation Depend on Nationalism," *East European Politics and Societies*, 4: 1, 1990, p. 115; see also Hubert Guindon, "Social Unrest, Social Class, and Quebec's Bureaucratic Revolution," in Bernard Blishen et al (eds.), *Canadian Society*, Toronto: Macmillan, 1968; Dale Posgate and Kenneth McRoberts, *Quebec: Social Change and Political Crisis*, Toronto: McClelland and Stewart, 1976.
5 Raymond Breton, "Institutional Completeness of Ethnic Communities and the Personal Relations of Immigrants," *American Journal of Sociology*, 70, 1964, pp. 193–205.
6 Richard Pipes, *The Formation of the Soviet Union*, New York: Athenaeum, 1974; Alexander Motyl, *Sovietology, Rationality, Nationality, Coming to Grips with Nationalism in the USSR*, New York: Columbia University Press, 1990, pp. 116–118.

96   Victor Zaslavsky

7 Gavriil Popov, "Kogda ishchut vragov ..." *Komsomolskaia pravda*, March 26, 1991, p. 3.
8 Zhores Medvedev, *Soviet Science*, New York: Norton, 1978, pp. 128–129 and 196–198; Mark Saroyan, "Beyond the Nation-State: Culture and Ethnic Politics in Soviet Transcaucasia," forthcoming.
9 Muriel Atkin, *Islam in Soviet Tadzhikistan*, Philadelphia: Foreign Policy Research Institute, 1990.
10 Edward Allworth, "The New Central Asians," in Edward Allworth (ed.), *Central Asia. 120 Years of Russian Rule*, Durham and London: Duke University Press, 1989, p. 572.
11 Viktor Kozlov, "Osobennosti etnodemograficheskikh problem v Srednei Azii i puti ikh resheniia," *Istoriia SSSR*, 1, 1988.
12 *Pravda*, July 6, 1990, p. 3.
13 Fedor Shelov-Kovedyaev, "Tretii lishnii," *Moskovskie novosti*, 34, 1990, p. 5.
14 Wlodzimierz Brus, "Political Pluralism and Markets in Communist Systems," in Susan Gross Solomon (ed.), *Pluralism in the Soviet Union*, New York: St. Martin's Press, 1982, p. 128.
15 Daniil Granin, "Chitaia Yeltsina," *Literaturnaia gazeta*, September 5, 1990, p. 10.
16 Galina Belaya, "Kul'tura epokhi raspada," *Moskovskie novosti*, 36, 1990, p. 14.
17 Adam Michnik, "The Two Faces of Europe," *New York Review of Books*, July 19, 1990, p. 7.
18 *Ibid.*
19 Sergei Chuprinin, "Situatsiia," *Znamia*, 1, 1990, p. 211.
20 Anatolii Strelianyi, "Pesni zapadnykh slavian," *Literaturnaia gazeta*, August 8, 1990, p. 3.
21 Adam Michnik, "The Two Faces of Europe," p. 7.
22 Victor Zaslavsky and Robert Brym, *Soviet-Jewish Emigration and Soviet Nationality Policy*, New York: St. Martin's Press, 1983, pp. 106–108.
23 Leokadia Drobizheva, "Etnicheskoe samosoznanie russkikh v usloviiakh perestroiki: ideologiia, politika, povsednevnoe povedenie," Paper presented at the World Congress on Soviet and East European Studies, Harrogate, July 21–26, 1990, p. 3.
24 Alexander Motyl, *Sovietology, Rationality, Nationality*, p. 167.
25 Roman Szporluk, "Dilemmas of Russian Nationalism," *Problems of Communism*, July–August, 1989, p. 17.
26 Vladimir Balakhonov, "Sokhranenie imperii ili samosokhranenie na puti natsional'nogo suvereniteta – glavnaia natsional'naia problema russkogo naroda segodnia," *Russkaia mysl*, June 23, 1989, p. 7.
27 *Ibid.*
28 Yuri Arutiunian, "Russians outside Russia," Paper presented at the Seventh Feltrinelli International Colloquium "Underdevelopment, Ethnic Conflict, and Nationalism in the Soviet Union," Cortona, Italy, May 16–18, 1991.
29 Mikhail Shirokii, "Perestroika, national'naia problema v SSSR i russkoe patrioticheskoe dvizhenie," *Vestnik Russkogo Khristianskogo Dvizheniia*, 153, 1988, p. 192.

30 Dmitry Volkogonov, "Tragedy of Freedom," *Moscow News*, 3, 1991, p. 3.
31 Alexander Prokhanov, "Zapiski konservatora," *Nash sovremennik*, 5, 1990, pp. 90–91.
32 Alexander Solzhenitsyn, "Kak nam obustroit' Rossiiu," *Literaturnaia gazeta*, September 18, 1990, pp. 3–6.
33 Marina Salie, "Pochemu russkoe demokraticheskoe dvizhenie 'styditsia' natsional'noi idei?" *Leningradskii literator*, February 9, 1990, p. 4.
34 Fedor Burlatsky, "K sovremennoi tsivilizatsii," *Literaturnaia gazeta*, September 5, 1990, p. 2.
35 John Dunlop, "Russian Nationalists Reach out to the Masses," *Working Papers in International Studies*, Stanford: Hoover Institution, 1990, pp. 30–31.
36 Igor Krupnik, in "Soiuz, Federatsiia, Konfederatsiia. Kruglyi stol," *Moskovskiie novosti*, 22, 1990, p. 9.
37 Galina Belaya, "Kul'tura epokhi raspada," p. 14.
38 Sergei Chuprinin, "Situatsiia," pp. 215–219.
39 Anatolii Strelianyi, "Pesni zapadnykh slavian," p. 3.
40 John Dunlop, "Ethnic Russians Confront a Loss of Empire," International Studies Working Paper, Stanford: The Hoover Institution, Stanford University, 1991, pp. 26–27.
41 Alexander Tsipko, "Vozmozhno li chudo?" *Sovetskaia kul'tura*, May 26, 1990, p. 3; Vera Tolz and Elizabeth Teague, "Tsipko Urges Ridding Soviet Society of Marxist Ideology," *Radio Liberty Report on the USSR*, 2: 23, 1990, pp. 4–5.
42 Ann Sheehy, "Fact Sheet on Declarations of Sovereignty," *Report on the USSR*, 2: 44, 1990, pp. 23–25.
43 *Kommersant*, 17, April 22–29, 1991, pp. 1–2.
44 Gavriil Popov, "Perspektivy i realii," *Ogonek*, 51, 1990, pp. 6–8; Valerii Tishkov, *Da uslyshitsia molitva moia*, Moscow: Institute of Ethnography, 1989.
45 Andrei Kozyrev, "Russia, In Its Own Voice," *The New York Times*, November 25, 1990, p. E11.
46 Alexander Tsipko, "Russia Comes to Life," *New Times*, April 2–8, 1991, p. 8.
47 Quoted in *The New York Times*, October 15, 1991, p. A3.
48 For a more detailed discussion see Victor Zaslavsky, "Nationalism and Democratic Transition in Postcommunist Societies," *Daedalus*, 121:2, Spring 1992, pp. 97–120.
49 Eduard Volodin, "Novaia Rossiia v meniaiushchemsia mire: realisticheskii prognoz," *Literaturnaia Rossiia*, January 26, 1990, pp. 3–4.
50 Evgenii Ambartsumov, "Politicheskaia fantaziia na irakskuiu temu," *Moskovskie novosti*, 33, 1990, p. 7.
51 Alexander Ivanchenko, "Agressiia bezobraznogo," *Literaturnaia gazeta*, December 26, 1990, p. 2.

5 Perestroika and the ethnic consciousness of Russians

LEOKADIA DROBIZHEVA

The years of perestroika completely undermined the theory of the merging (*sliianie*) of nations in the Soviet Union. The theory of the "melting pot" in the USA has also not withstood the test of time. Ethnic communities are increasingly making their demands, their interests, and their readiness to act in the name of these interests known throughout the world, and especially in the Soviet Union. Such interests were not only evident before the abortive coup attempt in August 1991, but had a direct impact on both the resolution and the consequences of the crisis.

The modern day articulation of demands by communities which are distinguishable by the size of their population, by their history, the type of territorial distribution, and their governmental and social status necessitates a critical reconsideration of our understanding of the word "nation." There has been an ongoing dispute among Soviet scholars over the utility of applying the concepts of "nation" and "nationality" to various ethnic groups.[1] In the Platform on Nationality Relations adopted by the Central Committee of the Communist Party in September 1989, both terms were employed.[2] Yet among Soviet ethnographers, especially after discussions during 1987–1989 with the British anthropologist Ernest Gellner, the notion that national ethnoses are communities which possess common ideas, values, and interests – that is, the characteristics of ethnic consciousness – became increasingly popular.[3]

The concept of ethnic consciousness includes one's self-identification as well as the popular perceptions concerning national characteristics that relate to one's own group (cognitive auto-stereotypes). Perceptions of a nation's origin, history, language, culture, traditions, standards of behavior, customs, and arts determine the character of these auto-stereotypes. All of these notions can be related to the image of a collective "we." In addition, the habitation, territory, and national sovereignty (if applicable) of an ethnos influences ethnic consciousness.

The emotional aspects of ethnic consciousness include pride in one's ethnic group achievements and a particular interest in this group's past.

It is ultimately necessary to single out the cognitive, emotional, and regulatory elements of ethnic consciousness in our socio-psychological research. Moreover, it is important to attach especial significance to those ethnic interests which can be seen as the "motor" by which people's activities are driven.[4]

National interests come into play when an ethnic group achieves statehood. Some of the titular nationalities of the union and autonomous republics have had their own statehood, as in the case of the Baltics. This statehood, though ephemeral, was nonetheless officially proclaimed. It became an integral part of the consciousness of Lithuanians, Georgians, Armenians, and others. In fact, the very use of the term "ethnicity" has sometimes been viewed as offensive to national pride. For example, one of the leaders of the Estonian National Movement, Mariju Lauristan, emphasized in her speeches that the national interests of Estonians do not simply encompass those cultural and linguistic matters which are usually perceived as related to ethnicity. Rather, these interests are broader and encompass questions of state independence and economic sovereignty, issues which were consistently at the top of the regional agenda until their successful resolution after the coup attempt in August.

It is important to note that Russian consciousness should be treated as ethnic rather than national. While Russians have their own sovereign statehood, 24 million Russians in the area of the former Soviet Union live outside the borders of the Russian Federation. The status of these Russians has been an important issue during interrepublican negotiations on the future shape of the Soviet Union. In order to examine the Russian group as a whole (in the Russian Federation as well as outside), it is most accurate to employ the notion of Russian ethnic consciousness.

Research carried out by the Institute of Ethnography's ethnosociologists in 1971–1972, 1979–1980, and 1987–1988 in Russia, Estonia, Moldova, Georgia, and Uzbekistan facilitates the comparative examination of ethnic consciousness and addresses the reasons for its upsurge throughout the Soviet Union.[5] Changes in the political and social situation in the Soviet Union permitted the Institute to take into consideration a rather large range of factors influencing this process.

National and ethnic interests have become more pronounced and have been perceived by the populace with increasing intensity, leading to a growth in ethnic consciousness. This growth was spurred on by an increase in the number of intellectuals and creative and scientific workers from every nationality of the Soviet Union who stress the importance of national identity. At the same time, the modern mass media enabled legitimate leaders to mobilize and rally populations around national ideas.

The growth of national consciousness was further influenced by the political situation, as well as by the frequent appeals to the national idea by political groups, parties, and social movements. It is thus of paramount importance to single out ideology, politics, and individual everyday behavior when considering problems connected with Russian national and ethnic consciousness.

In the 1970s and the early 1980s, and even in the first two to three years of perestroika itself, the ideology of the Russian patriotic movements had little influence upon mass public consciousness. As a rule, only a part of the humanitarian intelligentsia was aware of the ideological struggle between the magazines *Molodaia gvardiia* and *Novyi mir* in 1969–1970[6] or of the controversies over "The Lay of the Host of Igor," and Olzhas Suleymenov's *Az i ia* during the mid-1970s.[7]

The mass consciousness of the majority of Russians was relatively tranquil during the 1970s, and inter-ethnic attitudes towards the other nations of the Soviet Union were neutral or favorable. According to the findings of ethno-sociological studies carried out in the 1970s in Russian cities (such as Leningrad [now St. Petersburg], Saratov, Kalinin, and Krasnodar), as well as in other Soviet cities (such as Tashkent and Kishinev), most Russians (over 80 percent of the population) in these cities were favorably disposed to other nations. The Russians did not feel as comfortable in Tallinn, and they were aware of national competitiveness in Tiflis, but no upsurge of Russian consciousness was evident. At that time, over 70 percent of the Russian intelligentsia were favorably disposed towards other ethnic groups.

Wherever they lived, whether in their own ethnic surroundings or amidst other nations, Russians usually identified themselves as a nation primarily on the basis of common language. In Russian cities, as well as in Tiflis and Kishinev, most Russians (some two-thirds) believed that it was primarily language which united them. After that they most frequently identified themselves in terms of shared traditions and customs, and then, thirdly, by their professional culture. Common traits of character and history were the fourth and fifth most important factors (depending on the groups polled), and the place of residence and physical appearance ranked sixth or seventh.

Georgians, Moldovans, and Estonians attached much greater importance to historical literature than did Russians. Russians rated historical books fourth or fifth among books in all categories. Only books on World War II received a high rating among Russians. From 25 to 60 percent of Russian respondents named some feature, such as language or culture, which they believed to be essential to ethnic consciousness (for Georgian, Moldovan, and Estonian respondents this ranged from 70 to 80 percent). Some 25 percent of the Russian respondents did not name any particular trait common for all Russians as a whole, or they had difficulties in answering the question.

At the same time, even before the recent upsurge of national movements, an imperial mentality was widespread among Russians. This mentality was obvious not only in ideology and politics, but also characterized the Russian popular mind. For example, in response to a question on what they considered to be the "motherland" in the late 1970s and the early 1980s, 80 percent of Georgians and Uzbeks named their own republics, whereas Russians, regardless of where they lived (Moscow, Kishinev, or Tashkent), in most cases (70 per cent or more) named the Soviet Union as their motherland.[8]

Under the conditions of perestroika, and heightened by the explosion of national feeling which first occurred among the non-Russian peoples, an imperial mass national consciousness (i.e., new conceptions of their territory and of their native land) became a rallying point for Russians. This explosion of Russian national consciousness could have been predicted before perestroika. In the second half of the 1970s, and particularly in the 1980s, Russians felt that significant changes in their relations with other peoples of the Soviet Union were taking place. These changes were connected with two important circumstances.

First, since the late 1970s, Russians have been progressively confronted with non-Russian peoples whose relative socio-cultural potential has steadily increased and who increasingly viewed themselves as equal partners with Russians. Despite the harm done by the Stalin–Brezhnev regime to all non-Russian nationalities, the vast majority of the non-Russian population has become educated, and a large intelligentsia capable of expressing national interests has been created. This is not unprecedented. Situations where the social status of territorially contiguous ethnic communities is changing have led to the aggravation of national contradictions around the globe, as conflicts between English- and French-speaking Canadians, or between the Flemish and Walloons in Belgium remind us. When one ethnic community begins to catch up with another, economically, socially, and culturally further developed nation, the first community always articulates new demands, while the second becomes increasingly anxious about the loss of its former status. This type of social situation was characteristic of the Soviet Union in the 1970s and 1980s, whereas other developed and urbanized countries underwent such processes in the late 1960s and the early 1970s.

Second, the growing dissatisfaction with the worsening economic situation in the republics, along with the general political and moral decay in the country (particularly obvious in the last years of Brezhnev's and Chernenko's rule), was directed against the all-Union center. The center was in turn identified with Russians. As a result, it was natural to expect a Russian nationalist reaction. After all, Russians believed that they also suffered from the unfortunate consequences of the administrative-command system.

The events connected with perestroika introduced two essentially new factors affecting the growth of Russian national consciousness. The first factor was the extraordinary growth of national movements and inter-ethnic conflicts in the Baltic republics, Moldova, Georgia, Armenia, Azerbaijan, Ukraine, and Belorussia. Attempts to achieve Soviet republic status in the autonomous republics of Tataria, Bashkiria, Yakutia, Tuva, and Buryatia also contributed to this growth. This first provoked a defensive reaction, but with time this reaction was transformed into a more belligerent and offensive stance. The Russians attempted to consolidate as a group so as to disassociate themselves from the accusations which were directed at the center and the administrative-command system.

At the same time, the national movements in the periphery brought about a psychological chain-reaction among Russians, and some began to expropriate the tactics of the non-Russian groups by creating their own organizations, such as the Interfronts and the workers' collectives. These events took place in an atmosphere of frustration and high emotional tension. Stock phrases about invaders and rootless migrants and the adoption in the non-Russian republican parliaments of legislation dealing with the official language and citizenship not only wounded Russian national feelings in these republics, but also led to the consolidation of Russians in the Russian Federation.

The second factor connected with perestroika that drastically affected Russian national consciousness is the aggravation of the socio-political confrontation in the Soviet Union and in the Russian Federation itself. Conservatives and radicals were both forced to appeal to the national idea and to use the national-patriotic feelings of Russians to attempt to obtain a popular majority in the Soviet Union. The abortive coup attempt demonstrated that the fate not only of Russians, but of perestroika and, by extension, of the entire international community, hinged on the outcome of this struggle.

In the first stages of perestroika, right up until 1989, the ideology and policies of Gorbachev's team and the so-called left radicals (such as the *Moscow Tribune* and the Interregional Deputies Group) were not, with rare exceptions, oriented towards national ideas. The liberal intelligentsia articulated the idea of the democratization of society. The Russian population eagerly awaited changes in the economy and moral regeneration. Yet the Russian national-patriotic movement was ideologically active and retained hope that it would someday become a political vanguard and gain mass support.

In the non-Russian republics, several movements raised issues of national and political importance, such as problems of sovereignty, economic independence, the priority of national culture, language, and the reevaluation of historic events which were seen as detrimental to national pride. In contrast, these issues were formulated differently in Russia at the beginning of perestroika. For example, the question of political sovereignty had never been raised. Discussions centered around the creation of the Communist Party of the Russian Federation, the establishment of a Russian Academy of Sciences and the creation of a Russian national capital. Russians as a whole, including Russian national-patriotic movements, were mostly concerned with ecology, the renewal of Russia's culture, and problems of historical memory.

Books by Victor Astafiev (*King Fish*, *The Sad Detective*, and *Place of Action*), Peter Proskurin (*Fate* and *Your Name*), Valentin Rasputin (*Fire*), and Victor Chivilikhin (*Memory*), written before perestroika, attracted the particular attention of the public, critics, mass media, and creative unions (such as the Union of Writers and the Union of Cinematographers) at the end of the 1980s.[9] As an author wrote in *Nash sovremennik*:

Wise people understand that to eliminate the whole nation, especially a nation like Russia, is impossible nowadays. But it's possible to try to break the nation by destroying its spirit and by depersonalizing its culture. This is possible if the nation is transformed into a crowd devoid of history.[10]

Rasputin said in 1987:

There are people who very much dislike Russia's return of memory. That is why these people are willing to use the words "memory" and "patriotism" as swear words.[11]

At that time the activities of the organization Pamyat ("Memory") were becoming more and more evident. This group, which had originally defended Russian culture, acquired scandalous notoriety under the leadership of the right-wing radical Dimitry Vasil'ev as it searched for "enemies" in the persons of "conspiring" Jews and "Freemasons." This contributed to the aggravation of anti-Semitic feelings, and Pamyat fanned Russian chauvinism. Newspapers such as *Komsomol'skaia pravda* and *Moskovskie novosti* openly opposed this movement. Yet it should also be noted that during the meetings which were being held in the course of the spring 1990 election campaign in Moscow, Pamyat could not gather more than one hundred supporters. Of course, this did not mean that some of Pamyat's ideas were not shared by larger portions of the population. This was true in St. Petersburg, where Pamyat meetings had a higher attendance and where their participants were more aggressive. Still, according to data obtained in December 1989 by the center of Applied Sociological Research, the percentage of people in Moscow prepared to struggle against non-Russians and "cosmopolitans" in favor of Russia came to only 5 percent.[12]

There were more ominous ideas concerning Russia's future which were advanced by the Russian patriotic movement. These included an emphasis on the uniqueness of Russian historical development, which rejected the feasibility of adopting Western economic models in Russia,[13] and a general hostility toward liberal-democratic tendencies. Such tendencies were explicitly attacked in periodicals such as *Nash sovremennik* (the circulation of the magazine doubled from 1987 to 1990), *Molodaia gvardiia*, and *Literaturnaia Rossiia*. Polls demonstrate, however, that the public at large simply was not aware of these disputes even in Moscow, where Pamyat was very active. Nonetheless, the historical consciousness of Russians was clearly increasing, manifesting itself particularly in the concern for protection of historical monuments. The majority of Muscovites, according to polls carried out by the USSR Academy of Sciences Institute of Ethnography, believed that the restoration of historical monuments should be funded in spite of the inadequate financing of the health care system and of housing shortages.[14]

The appeal to Russian patriotic feelings during political campaigns at the time of the 1989 elections to the USSR Congress of People's Deputies was widespread. At electoral meetings one could often hear: "Vote for so-and-so – he is a Russian." From 1989 to 1990, it became apparent that the democratic movement would have to employ Russian national ideas in order to appeal to Russians.

It is well known that clubs, unions, and national fronts which supported perestroika and the radical reforms first appeared in 1987. Such organizations were particularly active in 1988. By the end of 1989, there were close to fifty such organizations in Moscow, St. Petersburg, Yaroslavl, Kuibyshev, Sverdlovsk, Omsk, Chelyabinsk, Nizhnii Novgorod, and other cities. Their political and ideological orientations were dissimilar, but they had the idea of nationality in common, as evident in the Baltics and in Armenia. By October 1989, all attempts to create an All-Russian Popular Front had been unsuccessful. By the end of 1989, on the eve of the preparations for the elections of the RSFSR people's deputies, a Confederation of the Popular Fronts and Democratic Movements of Russia was founded. At that time, the idea of reviving Russia played an important role in national consolidation.

Simultaneously, informal Russian patriotic organizations such as "Otechestvo" (Fatherland), "Rossiia Molodaia" (Young Russia), "Nevskaia Bitva" (The Neva River Battle), "Rossiiskoe Obshchestvo Spravedlivosti" (Russian Society of Justice), "Tovarishchestvo Russkikh Khudozhnikov" (Association of Russian Artists), "Rossy," and five factions of Pamyat arose. The RSFSR Writers' Union was a stronghold of chauvinist Russian nationalism. Belligerent anti-Semitic declarations at the Sixth Plenum of the RSFSR Writers' Union Management Board evoked widespread alarm and prompted criticism of the event. The Writers' Union responded to these critics by sending a letter to the CPSU Central Committee asserting that charges that the Sixth Plenum was an "anti-Semitic sabbath" were a large-scale provocation. It argued further that the treatment of Pamyat as a "mighty" force was an exaggeration: "There exist in reality only some masqueraders, who in all events could not be recognized as the mouth-piece of the whole nation." The letter also alleged discrimination against Russians. Because of nationality conflicts and "baseless" accusations against Russians, the letter continued, Russians were in need of urgent and extraordinary help from the United Nations and the Security Council. The letter expressed one particularly ominous warning: "The moral blackmail of the patient and good-natured Russian people, ever sensitive to the misfortunes of their neighbors, a blackmail which hurts Russian national pride, has reached such a degree that the provocateurs should not count on Russian forgiveness and endurance." As far as the increasingly frequent Soviet contacts with Israel were concerned, the authors of the letter expressed their opinion that "the free import of Zionism into this country has become a threatening reality."[15] Rasputin delivered a speech in America, in which he appended his theory of a Masonic conspiracy to his previous positions, including the protection of the culture, historical memory, and environment of Russia.

The Russian national-patriotic movement was not ideologically homogenous. It included organizations dedicated to the revival of culture and to the morality of peoples – not only Russians, but also the other peoples of Russia. Four groups were of particular interest. "The Union for the Spiritual Regeneration of the Fatherland," a national-patriotic federation which included associations in Moscow, St. Petersburg, the Volga region, the Urals, Siberia, Belorussia, Ukraine, Kazakhstan, as well as representatives of the Russian Orthodox Church, became active in March 1989. In its political platform, the federation supported a socialist variant of perestroika. The St. Petersburg group "Spasenie" (Salvation) and its members could generally be described as cultural environmentalists. This group's actions were directed towards the rescue of historical and cultural monuments. The "Russkoe Znamia" (Russian Banner) society could also be classified as an historical-patriotic group. This group struggled for the reinstatement of Russian national symbols, such as flags and state insignia, the reestablishment of the old names of Russian cities, and the creation of a Russian Academy of Sciences. Finally, on the eve of the republic and local elections in the RSFSR, an "Association of Russian Artists" took the initiative to create the Joint Council of Russia (OSR), a group which included Russian patriotic groups, cultural and educational organizations, clubs, societies, funds, and fronts. The OSR also included the Interfronts of the Baltic republics and Moldova.[16]

Before the end of 1989, the national patriotic platform included demands for adhering to a specifically Russian path of development that would bring about a reversal of the harm which had been done to Russian culture, demography, and economy.[17] Since the end of 1989, new ideas have been added to this platform. These include the ideas of Russian sovereignty, economic and cultural independence, the reinstatement of the previous national name (Great Russians),[18] and a call for separatism.[19] The need to protect Russians in the non-Russian republics was actively discussed ("Not one hair should fall off anyone's head. Not one tear should drop. The Russian population shall not be held hostage by national and political intrigues").[20] Notably, the idea of employing the army as the defender of Russian statehood also arose.[21]

The Russian national idea had a growing impact on mass consciousness and on political life. The official publications of the Russian patriotic movement had a circulation of 1.5 million. According to the representatives of the Russian nationalist movement, there was a print run of 60 million copies of "russophobic" publications.[22] This charge ignored the fact that the national feelings and inclinations of Russians were also represented by Russian-oriented organs of the mass media, such as *Sovetskaia Rossiia*. A content analysis of *Sovetskaia Rossiia* demonstrates this fact. In comparison with 1957–1958, the frequency of the usage of the term "Russian patriotism" in this paper increased fivefold by the end of the 1980s, and the frequency of the usage of old Russian folklore terms fourfold.

Central Television created a special Russian channel. The popular magazine *Rodina* was handed over to the Russian Federation. In this way, the ideological influence of Russian national ideas increased by the spring of 1990. In December 1990, at the Seventh Congress of the Union of Russian Writers, calls were heard to publish (in conjunction with the army) a new weekly, one which would allegedly be more popular than *Ogonek*.

Gorbachev took Russian national-patriotic feelings and ideas into account long before the coup attempt. The invitation to Rasputin to participate in the Presidential Council was particularly significant. At meetings held by Congress and Supreme Soviet deputies, Rasputin threatened that Russia might secede from the USSR. The Russian national idea, as presented by chauvinistic movements, did not gain much currency among the population at large. Still, national feelings, especially after revelations of past abuses of power, corruption, and of the unbearable standards of living, had become so strained that populist explosions were seen as a real possibility by the Soviet leadership. This moment was a cardinal turning point in the role that Russian patriotic ideas played in the conduct of politics. During the RSFSR Congress of People's Deputies election campaigns and later during the meeting of the Congress in May 1990, the radical democratic movement finally incorporated these ideas, which had long been "knocking at the door."

Boris Yeltsin actively employed the idea of Russian sovereignty during his struggle for power. In the summer of 1990, during visits to various regions of the RSFSR, he proclaimed in a public address that "[w]e cannot go on living in such conditions. Seventy billion rubles are being taken from Russia. Where to?"[23] Other radical democrats, such as Galina Starovoiteva, condemned the harm by the totalitarian system to the Russian people and referred to the past repressions of the intelligentsia and peasantry. Russian national concepts, devoid of references to a peculiar path of Russian development or to "hidden enemies," began to help the cause of the democratic movement.

With the upheaval that accompanied perestroika, leaders of the central party apparatus increasingly appealed to national patriotism. This could be seen during Vadim Medvedev's speech at the Twenty-Eighth Congress of the CPSU: "The main task for today is to support the people's belief in perestroika ... For this purpose, the Party should rely on the deep-rooted patriotic feelings of our people and should be inspired by the idea of national restoration."[24]

As we have seen, the national-patriotic idea was actively used in the non-Russian republics in the programs of the National Fronts in Estonia, Lithuania, Latvia, Moldova, Ukraine ("Rukh") and by political groups in Georgia, Armenia, Azerbaijan, and Uzbekistan. In Russia, national ideas, particularly the idea of national sovereignty, radicalized the political situation at the beginning of the summer of 1990. At the Congress of the RSFSR People's Deputies, some thirty deputies spoke for the precedence of the Russian Republic's laws over the all-Union ones. Even more deputies supported economic sovereignty and independence. The majority of delegates then voted for the priority of the republic's laws over all-Union legislation, and for the right to control Russian resources. Indeed, the Russian government was repeating actions which had been severely criticized by the Presidium of the Supreme Soviet of the USSR only two years earlier, when such measures had been adopted by the Baltic republics, Georgia, Moldova, and Azerbaijan.

The adoption of the Declaration of Russia's Sovereignty, notwithstanding the fact that the declaration had been shortened and smoothed over, was of principal importance. This adoption meant that the relations between the republics and the center were to change fundamentally. Such relations could now conceivably be based not on the so-called "vertical" agreements between the center and the republics, but on "horizontal" agreements between the republics, agreements which would be more important and reliable since they would be based on the free choice and direct interests of the republics themselves. Such agreements were indeed signed in the summer of 1990 between the Russian Federation and the Baltic republics. Following this example, other republics also reached agreements, such as Azerbaijan and Belorussia, Azerbaijan and Georgia, and Moldova and Latvia.

But this was only one political trend. Another trend was connected with attempts to exploit national-patriotic feelings by the forces opposing perestroika. Supporters of right-wing trends in the government apparatus, in the Communist Party, and in the army tried to use the national feelings, and sometimes the national prejudices, of Russians, who found themselves in a difficult economic situation and who were unprepared for political pluralism, for their own ends. The Initiative Congress of the Communists of Russia in St. Petersburg in 1990, which was soon followed by the Congress of the Communist Party of the RSFSR, signified the open cooperation of the relatively unpopular Russian chauvinist movement with the conservative wing of the CPSU.

The newly founded Republican People's Party of Russia proclaimed in its program that it supported "freedom for national life, cooperation and equal dialogue between all of the nationalities inhabiting the country, and resolutely opposes any violence, chauvinism, or national intolerance." Yet at the same time, it called for the restoration of "Russian Statehood, destroyed in 1917, for the right of the Russian people to an independent State within the boundaries of the RSFSR, and for the foundation of national schools, theaters ... and mass media."[25] Some of the articles also opposed separatism in the autonomous republics within Russia. In a number of cities, Russian patriotic groups cooperated with the "Ob'edinennyi Front Trudiashchikhsia" (United Front of Toilers, or OFT) to defend the rights of the Russian-speaking population in the non-Russian republics. This was possible because the political aims of the Interfronts and OFT are very similar.

In sum, we have seen, an ideological convergence between left and right on national issues which is connected with the development of Russian ethnic consciousness, but also a political confrontation between the two tendencies which had become manifest by the autumn of 1990. This political confrontation led to growing tensions between the conservative wing of the CPSU and Russian patriotic movement on the one hand, and the Bloc of Democratic Russia, which tried to radicalize the situation, on the other hand. The difficult victory of the political center at the Twenty-Eighth Congress of the CPSU did not alleviate these tensions.

Factors affecting the intensification of Russian national consciousness, strains in the political situation, and the further aggravation of the economic situation influenced both the inter-ethnic attitudes of Russians and their everyday behavior. On the one hand, the growth of ethnocentrism among Russians, who increasingly concentrated on their own national interests, was evident. A poll of 1,100 Muscovites in November 1990, conducted by the USSR Academy of Sciences' Institute of Ethnography and Anthropology, found that 44 percent supported the idea of maintaining the union, 25 percent favored the secession of the RSFSR from the USSR, and 25 percent were undecided. Some 10 percent favored preserving the union through economic sanctions, while a negligible 0.5 percent supported the use of military force to preserve the territorial integrity of the USSR.

On the other hand, sociological investigations at the end of the 1980s showed that the attitudes of Russians towards other nationalities took a negative turn, not only in the non-Russian republics, but in Russia proper. Ethnosociological studies carried out in the 1970s had shown that the proportion of negative inter-ethnic attitudes of Russians towards business and family contacts were no more than 10–15 percent, and the proportion of combined negative attitudes towards various inter-ethnic contacts proved to be no more than 2–8 percent. Such attitudes were particularly characteristic of unskilled, less-educated, or less-urbanized individuals. Negative inter-ethnic attitudes in the spheres of business and professional activities were specifically characteristic of the humanitarian intelligentsia in big cities (such as St. Petersburg). Those attitudes changed significantly over the next decade. According to polls at the end of the 1980s and expert data assessment, the proportion of Russians with ethnic prejudices has risen more than one-and-a-half to two times.

Anti-Semitic feelings were also on the rise in Russia. Opinion polls carried out by a joint Soviet–American team of socio-ethnologists in 1990 showed that such feelings could be detected among one-fifth to one-third of the residents of Moscow and St. Petersburg, where anti-Semitism was most pronounced. Anti-Semitic feelings were likewise observed in Belorussia.

In Russia, rising anti-Azerbaijani and anti-Armenian feelings were connected with the flow of refugees. In some regions of the Russian Federation, such as Yakutia, Buryatia, and Tuva, relations between Russians and the indigenous nationalities have become increasingly strained. For example, in Tuva sociological polls showed that up to 90 percent of the Russian population felt ethnic pressure. This pressure was so serious that people were ready to migrate to Russian regions.[26] The number of Russians who may not have firm negative inter-ethnic attitudes, but who are still biased against people of other nationalities, has grown. It is quite natural also that the national consciousness of such people is becoming more pronounced.

The events of August 1991 became the basis for a new rise in Russian self-identification. Even as he defended democracy, Yeltsin appealed to the ethnic feelings of Russians. The White House became a symbol of Russian freedom. During a victory demonstration on August 24, the three-colored Russian flag was raised over the Parliament Building, Yeltsin revealed a new coat-of-arms for Russia and renewed the Order of Saint George. One could sense the feelings of Russian pride at the demonstrations of August 20 and 24. The mass consciousness of Russians was freed from any feelings of guilt over the past.

But when, after the putsch, Kazakhstan, Ukraine, and Uzbekistan declared independence, the ethnocentrism of Russians increased. Even Yeltsin's aides claimed that secession from the union would only occur after the resolution of territorial issues. Anatoly Sobchak and Alexander Rutskoi were forced to defuse the tension that arose by taking trips to Kazakhstan and Ukraine.

A unique situation emerged – the "international" team of democrats around Yeltsin (including the Ukrainian Sergei Stankevich, the Chechen Ruslan Khasbulatov, and the Greek Gavriil Popov) feared the rise of nationalism in the republics, and they began to proclaim the same ideology as the former centralists in the government. The new Russian Constitution, which does not recognize the independence of the Tatars or of the Chechen, is evidence of the adoption of the ideas of some elements in the national-patriotic movements by various officials in the new Russian state apparatus.

These issues are likely to become even more acute in the aftermath of the August coup attempt. On the one hand, the decentralization of the political apparatus will enhance the opportunities for many ethnic groups to fulfill their dreams of national statehood – indeed, such dreams have now been realized in the Baltic. Yet during periods of political upheaval and economic crises, national prejudices have always increased. Many critical problems, such as the issue of migration and the status of groups living outside their national boundaries, are the product of long-term processes that will take the coordinated efforts of the representatives of different ethnic groups to resolve. Interethnic relations will not be harmonized until after the stabilization of the political and economic situation and the adoption of democratic forms of government.

NOTES

This text was translated by Victor Zaslavsky and Philip Goldman.

1 Yulian Bromley, former director of the Institute of Ethnography, insisted that both terms should be used as they reflected different levels of various nations' development. Yet his application of the terms "nation" and "nationality" was purely subjective. Such differentiation had been dictated by the conditions of Stalin's nationality policy. Mikhail Kryukov was one of the first who under conditions of perestroika doubted the reliability of the criteria used for telling nations from nationalities.

2 "Natsional'naia politika partii v sovremennykh usloviiakh," (Platforma KPSS), *Pravda*, September 24, 1989.

3 For example, Valerii Tishkov, "O kontseptsii perestroiki natsional'nykh otnoshenii v SSSR," *Sovetskaia etnografiia*, 1989, no. 1, pp. 76–77. In the 1970–1980s, ethnic consciousness was broadly examined by Soviet historiographers. These views were presented in Yulian Bromley's book, *Ocherki teorii etnosa* (Moscow, 1983). For Gellner's views, see Ernest Gellner, *Nations and nationalism* (Ithaca, Cornell University Press, 1983).

4 Leokadia Drobizheva, "Natsional'noe samosoznanie: baza formirovaniia i sotsial'no-kul'turnye stimuly razvitiia," *Sovetskaia etnografiia*, 1985, no. 5; the chapter "Kul'tura i natsional'noe samosoznanie" of the book by Yuri Arutiunian and Leokadia Drobizheva, *Mnogoobrazie kul'turnoi zhizni narodov SSSR*, Moscow, 1987.

5 I am also doing research on ethnic consciousness and inter-ethnic relations.

6 See *Molodaia gvardiia*, 1970, no. 8; *Ogonek*, 1969, no. 30; *Literaturnaia Rossiia*, August 1, 1969; *Sovetskaia Rossiia*, August 3, 1969; *Literaturnaia gazeta*, August 27, 1969; *Novyi mir*, 1969, no. 7; *Kommunist*, 1970, no. 15.

7 *Zvezda*, 1976, no. 6; *Molodaia gvardiia*, 1975, no. 10.

8 In Tallinn, however, 53 percent of Russian respondents named the USSR and 25 percent named Estonia.

9 In a study of readers' preferences in Moscow, it was found that there were more than 100 people waiting to get Astafiev's book, *The Sad Detective*, in one of Moscow's libraries – as many as those waiting for Daniil Granin's book *Zubr* – the most popular book at that time.

10 Mikhail Dunayev, "Rokovaia muzyka," *Nash sovremennik*, 1988, no. 1, pp. 163–164.

11 Valentin Rasputin, "Zhertvovat' soboi dlia pravdy," *Nash sovremennik*, 1987, no. 2, p. 171.

12 Nine-hundred people were polled by telephone. See *Argumenty i fakty*, 1990, no. 7, p. 6.

13 Apollon Kuzmin, "K kakomu khramu ishchem my dorogu?" *Nash sovremennik*, 1988, no. 3.

14 Two thousand people were chosen from the official list of electors.

15 *Literaturnaia Rossiia*, 1990, no. 9.

16 *Neformal'naia Rossiia*, Moscow, 1990, p. 307.

17 *Nash sovremennik*, 1990, no. 1, pp. 168–176; no. 2, pp. 9–11; no. 3, p. 88; no. 4, p. 140.

18 See Arseny Gulyga, "Russkii vopros," *Nash sovremennik*, 1990, no. 1, pp. 168–176.
19 Alexander Prokhanov, "Zametki konservatora," *Nash sovremennik*, 1990, no. 5, p. 103.
20 *Ibid.*, p. 91.
21 *Ibid.*, p. 98. Karem Rash, "Armiia i kul'tura," *Nash sovremennik*, 1990, no. 5, p. 103.
22 *Literaturnaia Rossiia*, 1990, no. 9.
23 Speech at meeting in Karaganda, August 18, 1990.
24 *Pravda*, July 4, 1990, p. 2.
25 *Literaturnaia Rossiia*, 1990, no. 16, p. 6.
26 TV program "Vremya," August 20, 1990.

6 Nationality policies in the period of perestroika: some comments from a political actor

GALINA STAROVOITEVA

The years of perestroika, especially the last two or three years, were marked by an unprecedented upsurge of national movements, national agitations, and conflict. These national movements arose for different reasons throughout the Soviet Union. In some areas, like the Baltic states, national movements have been distinguished by the striving for the establishment of state independence, and they developed in the framework of a constitutional process – even, to some extent, after the abortive coup in August 1991. In other regions, particularly in Central Asia and the Caucasus, or on the border line dividing the Islamic and Christian worlds, nationality conflicts generally took a violent form, as demonstrated by the clashes between Armenia and Azerbaijan. They began with the unrest of December 1986 in Alma-Ata, which was followed by outbreaks in Nagorno-Karabakh in 1988. These events were completely unexpected by the public, by experts on nationalities, by the press, and by political authorities. Why was this the case?

Soviet social science, always obedient to authority, began to develop the concept of the Soviet people as a new historical community in the late 1960s. This was only a smoke-screen to hide the attempts at the forced and accelerated assimilation of non-Russian nationalities. This assimilation was not initiated by the Russian people, who were themselves subject to a considerable de-ethnocization. Rather, the attempted assimilation came from the Soviet political system, which sought to create a homogeneous supra-ethnic community. In fact, certain features of everyday life and behavior had become characteristic of the entire Soviet population. Yet these features were very superficial among the non-Russian nationalities. Supra-national behavioral and ideological stereotypes took deeper root among the Russian people, who became "less ethnic" as a result.

The Soviet propaganda apparatus used Stalin's definition of a nation to demonstrate the fact that a new Soviet community had arisen on the basis of a common territory, language, economic life, culture, and national psychology. It insisted that the peoples of the Soviet Union had already merged into one supra-national community – the Soviet people. Indeed, politicians themselves believed in their own propaganda – as Marx once noted, the label fools both the buyer and the merchant. In reality, however, the deep structures of different nations remained quite distinct even after exposure to the Soviet way of life.

As society came to reject the false slogans of the Soviet regime, a spiritual vacuum developed and people began to turn to traditional values, above all to family and nation, in search of a deeper meaning to their lives. In the course of perestroika, when people had the opportunity to seek liberation from totalitarianism, national movements became a basis for the rise and development of civil society.

The national idea effectively mobilizes social movements, as can be seen throughout Europe: the process of German unification and the attempt to unify the two artificially separated parts of Armenia are both examples of its power. Nationalism is now especially potent in the countries of Eastern Europe, and it ultimately spread to the Soviet republics.

According to Article 70 of the Soviet Constitution, the republics have always been sovereign states. But this sovereignty has never been a political reality until today, when this constitutional arrangement unexpectedly achieved new relevance, both before and after the August coup, most strikingly in the Baltic states. The sudden upsurge in nationalism was misunderstood by Soviet social science as well as by the mass media. Two immediate explanations were advanced – one explaining nationalism in terms of "vulgar economism," while the second promoted "conspiracy" theories.

According to vulgar economism, national movements are nothing but socio-economic movements in disguise. National conflicts are the product of economic backwardness and poverty. To some extent, this may indeed be the case. National conflicts are usually more acute in areas with a low standard of living and which are experiencing growing shortages of bread, meats, and consumer goods. Thus, at the beginning of the Nagorno-Karabakh crisis one often heard: "What is their problem? Don't they have enough meat over there?" As a result, the first reaction of the Soviet government to the Karabakh crisis was a decree by the USSR Council of Ministers to accelerate the socio-economic development of the Nagorno-Karabakh region. Subsequent aid sent to the area was thwarted by rail blockades, even though economic assistance would not have been a solution to the conflict.

One need only consider the experiences of other parts of the world: there is no food rationing in Ulster, but ethnic conflict has been going on there for more than a decade.

The "conspiracy" theory argues that national movements do not appear spontaneously. According to this conception, they are the products of "dark forces and internal conspiracies," including the work of Masons, Jews, or foreign agents. During the Armenian disturbances, the Mafia and Armenian nationalists residing abroad were often blamed for provoking the conflict. Such conspiratorial ideas are primitive and can be traced to the most archaic levels of human consciousness: the misfortunes of ancient peoples were often blamed on magicians from neighboring tribes.

These two approaches are fundamentally flawed. In reality, people lost confidence in the capacity of the central government to resolve national conflicts after Moscow demonstrated that it had no real plan for addressing the conflicts in Nagorno-Karabakh or in any other region. This strengthened separatist tendencies and led to an increase in nationalist violence throughout the Soviet Union. The Baltic populations watched the events in Nagorno-Karabakh very carefully. The failure of central leadership in Nagorno-Karabakh prompted these populations to seek a solution to their problems within the framework of self-determination, which had already been formally granted by the constitution. Separatism spread throughout the Soviet Union and even arose in the autonomous republics of the Russian Federation, which began to press aggressively for sovereignty.

The unity of any state is dependent on two basic factors: an integrated economic system (market or command) and a uniform ideological system, whether political, nationalist or religious. Both have been destroyed in the Soviet Union. In this turbulent period following the disintegration of the former apparatus after the August coup, economic and ideological integration can occur only on the foundation of civil society. It is important to note that the Soviet nations already possess many features characteristic of an emerging civil society. These include common physical attributes, the prevalence of horizontal social ties over vertical hierarchical subordination, and the role of historical memory. Also, the individual's ethnic and social identification has been facilitated by cultural and historical continuity, while public opinion has regulated socially meaningful forms of individual action.

Some of the nations of the former Soviet Union wish to join a United Europe, and one hears frequent references to a "common European home." In order to accomplish this, however, they must be integrated on the basis of democratic principles. In the absence of democratic integration, there is no reason why some of the remaining republics cannot join the EC on their own. The area of the former Soviet Union is extremely heterogeneous. There are peoples with religions that range from the Christian (Catholic, Protestant, and Orthodox) to the Islamic (Shi'ite and Sunni), Judaic, Buddhist, and pagan traditions. In those regions where religion does not play a major role, cultural and religious practices from previous centuries nevertheless shape the national psychology.

As democrats confronting a new Soviet order, we must recognize that all peoples are equal and that each culture makes a distinct and valuable contribution to the common culture of mankind. The principle of cultural relativism demands that we accept the equal worth of every nation on this planet. Yet the practical politician must recognize the fact that different religious and historical traditions affect the receptivity of people to a transition to democracy.

Despite the assertions of the pre-coup Soviet leadership that it sought a democratic and pluralist approach to solving problems, state policies differed little from those of the Stalin epoch. After five years of perestroika, we did not develop any realistic domestic strategy to deal with the national problem. As before, the mentality of the Soviet leadership was dominated by a Byzantine tradition which gave priority to the state over the community or individual.

This was clearly evident at the September 1989 Central Committee Plenum which adopted a Party platform on Soviet nationality relations. Discussions at the Plenum were dominated by a statist approach to nationality problems: the state's interests took precedence over the interests of any ethnic group. To cite just one example, during discussions on the return of the Crimean Tatars and Soviet Germans to their historical homelands, the need for justice and full rehabilitation was subordinated to the argument that any measures must first take the Soviet state's interests into account, despite the fact that these nations were punished and deported in the absence of any crime on their part whatsoever. This statist approach was originally responsible for the repression of the Crimean Tatar movement, and for the mass emigration of Soviet Germans, a group which could have contributed much to Soviet development.

The Meskhetian Turks are another minority that were denied the opportunity to return to their ethnic homeland. Driven by inter-ethnic violence out of Uzbekistan, where they were deported by the Stalinist government in the first place, they are now scattered around the Soviet Union, since both the central government and the Georgian leadership did not permit their return to Georgia.

Officials in Moscow demonstrated a continual reluctance to correct historical injustices, and their statist approach contributed to new ones. Troops from the Ministry of Internal Affairs, lacking a real strategy for dealing with inter-ethnic conflict, pressured Armenians in Nagorno-Karabakh to move from settlements where they had resided for centuries, thus increasing the overall number of Soviet refugees fleeing from ethnic violence to 700,000. It is important to emphasize that these deportations were not the direct result of pressures from the Azerbaijani population.

The failures of the government also contributed to the rise of anti-Semitism, which was not only a social manifestation, but could be directly traced to the state. We are now facing the possibility of a massive complete Jewish emigration from the area of the former Soviet Union. Soviet Jews constitute almost two million people, and they have a tremendous cultural potential. Today they feel insecure because of outbursts by so-called patriotic movements that go un-punished. Not only has anti-Semitic propaganda been widespread in periodicals such as *Molodaia gvardiia* and *Nash sovremennik*, but Jews feel that the authorities did not provide sufficient protection from pogroms.

Anti-Semitic groups have failed to gain broad popular support. Thus, during the March 1990 elections to the Russian Parliament, the first official multi-party elections in seventy years, deputies were selec-ted from two lists. The Bloc of Democratic Russia counterpoised its list to a list of "patriotic" candidates, many of whom were openly anti-Semitic. Sociological surveys revealed that in different regions of the country, the patriotic group was supported, on average, by 8–10 percent of the population. While this is more support than Hitler received at the beginning of the 1920s, it should be emphasized that the bloc of "patriots" suffered a decisive defeat. Even a popular and famous artist like Iliia Glazunov, known for his involvement with this bloc, lost to a completely unknown representative from the group "Democratic Russia." In spite of this, several supporters of the patriotic forces were subsequently named members of Gorbachev's Presidential Council, while not one deputy from the "Democratic Russia" bloc was appointed to this body.

An analysis of Soviet nationality relations cannot avoid the unique and paradoxical position of Russians within the area of the former

Soviet Union. Russians constitute a majority of the overall population, and have played a dominant role in the political elite at both the union and republican level. As a rule, the second secretary of the Communist Party of a non-Russian republic was always Russian, and many other important positions, especially in the coercive apparatus, were also held by Russians. The traditional hegemony of the Russian language was quite clear. The central press, radio, and television broadcasts, higher educational organs, and governmental bodies all used Russian. At the same time, Russians suffered as much as non-Russians from the Stalinist repressions. The Russian people lost such important groups as the aristocracy, the merchant class, military officers, and the clergy. Russian peasants were decimated by the collectivization drive. As a result, the image of the Russian people presented in the works of great Russian authors, such as Chekhov, Tolstoy, and Dostoevsky, no longer corresponds to the contemporary Russian national character.

The Russian population is spread out across vast expanses of the country, and Russians have poor means of communicating with one another. They are stratified into groups with different social character-istics, and it is difficult to assess their readiness to undertake major political and economic reforms. We do know that ethnic Russian consciousness has its own peculiarities. Social thinkers such as Nikolai Berdyaev observed that Russians have their own ways of organizing ideas and their own mentality, and stressed the influence of geogra-phic space on the Russian national character. It is true that geography influenced Russian ethnic consciousness even more than history. The great power mentality of Russians has always been associated with a strong government, control over immense territory, and with Russian chauvinism.

A brief review of Soviet nationality problems reveals the complexity which political reformists face. The Soviet Union has been the last empire to undergo the world-wide process of decolonization which has been going on since the end of World War II. Soviet decoloniz-ation, however, encounters its own specific difficulties. The Soviet republics are territorially contiguous, and a massive internal migration has taken place within the Soviet Union. As a result, some 25 million Russians live outside the boundaries of the Russian republic. There-fore, the British transition from empire to commonwealth is a less relevant example for the Soviet Union than French decolonization, with its evacuation of approximately one million French citizens from Algeria. In addition, the imperial mentality of Russians mentioned above represents another obstacle to decolonization. Finally, Soviet decolonization will ultimately require a willingness to change the republics' arbitrarily drawn borders, though any changes will have to be made in a civilized and rational manner. The experience of German unification might serve as a good example.

In short, the central government did not adequately recognize the importance of the nationality problem and failed to introduce a comprehensive and realistic nationality policy. A constitutional approach to national problems was not seriously attempted. Gorbachev's pre-coup insistence on a new Union Treaty would have required alterations in territorial boundaries, and a number of union republics openly refused to sign the document, viewing it as a threat to their sovereignty. Several autonomous republics also balked at supporting the treaty, as it gave the union republics the right to determine the nature of their internal administrative apparatuses. In the future, economic integration will ultimately have to precede political integration. This is why a Union Treaty as originally conceived by Gorbachev is not the correct approach. Not a new Union Treaty, but a Treaty on a community of sovereign republics must be agreed upon. Conflicts would then be resolved in the parliaments rather than on the streets.

A treaty on a community of sovereign republics would include the following provisions. First, it would reject the formal hierarchical division of major ethnic groups into categories of union republics, autonomous republics, autonomous provinces, and national districts, and would give all peoples equal status and direct access to the center. Every nationality would also have been equal in cultural and human rights. Second, authority would be delegated from the bottom up. Each subject of the union would determine its own level of sovereignty, and decide which functions to delegate to the center. Sovereignty is meaningless without one's own army, security service, information and banking services, and so forth. Yet some republics might delegate questions of international trade, defense, postal services, monetary functions, or transport to the center while retaining other functions themselves. These would be matters to be decided by each member of the federation. Third, it would allow for the emergence of new political entities for nationalities demanding their own statehood, such as the Gagauz, the Volga Germans, the Crimean Tatars, the Kurds, and other groups. By allowing for new political entities to arise, new ethnic state formations might emerge in Azerbaijan, Buryatia, Ossetia, and the problems in these regions would be alleviated. Fourth, it would allow for new levels of integration, such as sub-federations which might arise from treaties concluded between two or more republics, bypassing the center. As a result, a confederation would emerge in which Nagorno-Karabakh could conclude its own agreements with Armenia. Finally, it would be necessary to strengthen the sovereignty of the Russian Federation itself by adopting a new federal treaty for the republic. The Russian Federation is currently a federation within a federation, and guarantees must be given to regions such as Tataria, Bashkiria, and the northern Caucasus. In addition, the Russian and Soviet capitals should be divided. Moscow could remain the capital of Russia, and a large city close to the geographic center of the Soviet Union (perhaps in the Urals or Siberia) might serve as the federal capital.

The March 1991 referendum on the preservation of the union demonstrated that the Soviet government was pursuing increased centralization. Despite the refusal of six republics to participate in the referendum, it seemed clear that the vote would be used to legitimate the forced preservation of the union. Some experts were convinced that the referendum would allow the Soviet president to gather both legislative and executive power into his hands in order to impose an authoritarian regime with some similarities to Pinochet's Chile, with political repression accompanying a move towards a market economy. Yet the Soviet people were politically aware, and not prepared to tolerate repressive means towards a supposedly "liberal" end. The coup's "Committee of Eight," which asserted its willingness to continue the policies of perestroika, was clearly unaware of this state of affairs.

It is sometimes alleged that the Soviet Union's decentralization ran against the general trends toward integration observable in the rest of the world. We were hoping to move from a unitary state to a confederation, while greater unification is on the European agenda. But it should not be forgotten that ours was an artificially developed state, founded on violence. A confederation would mean real sovereignty or even independence for the subjects of this formerly unitarian state. European integration and Soviet decolonization should thus be viewed as movements toward the same point from opposite ends of the spectrum.

NOTE

This text was translated by Victor Zaslavsky, James Chavin, and Philip Goldman.

Index

25–9, 39, 49, 54, 65, 86, 88–9, 102, 106, 108; and attitude toward Russians, 8, 34, 50–1, 63–4; and foreign economic relations, 19, 66; independence or secession of, 9, 17, 64, 93, 111
Union for the Spiritual Regeneration of the Fatherland, 106
Union of Cinematographers, 103
Union of Soviet Socialist Republics (USSR), *see* Soviet Union
Union of Writers (in various republics), 50, 55, 82, 94, 103, 105, 107; *see also* Congress of Soviet Writers
Union Treaty, 11–12, 15, 62–4, 75, 77, 87, 90–1, 120
United Nations (UN), 16, 105
United States of America, 17–18, 62, 98; and policy towards USSR and new nations, 17–18
United Workers' Front (United Front of Toilers – OFT), 85, 94, 109
Uzbekistan/Uzbek people, 7, 16, 36–7, 40, 51, 77, 90, 108, 111, 117, *see also* Central Asia; Communist party of, 31, 40, 78

Valjas, Vaino, 36

Vasiyev, Dimitry, 104
Vezirov, Abdu-Rakhman Khalil, 39
Vilnius, 36, 63
Vladivostok, 83
Volga Germans, 30, 120, *see also* Germans
Volga Tatars, 26, 51
Volkogonov, Dmitry, 85
Volodin, Eduard, 94

West, 17–20, 104, *see also* Europe, United States; and ties with new nations, 17–20, 64, 75, 92
working class, 25, 27–8; *see also* ethnicity
World War II, 30, 49, 101

Yakovlev, Aleksander, 33
Yakutia, 102, 110
Yanayev, Gennadi, 15
Yarin, Veniamin, 87
Yavlinsky, Grigory, 92
Yeltsin, Boris, 8, 12, 15–17, 41, 58, 63–4, 87, 90–2, 107, 110–11
Young Russia ("Rossiia Molodaia"), 105
Yugoslavia, 41

Zaslavsky, Victor, 2, 7, 9